Hour Four

Hour Four

Surviving the Earthquake in Haiti

Owen Spears

Table of Contents

To all those who give beyond their means

Marc and Lucianna

Five dollars from each book will go to Haiti Arise, a charity based in Haiti.

iii

1. Let's Go To Haiti

A couple of soldiers came to guide all of us on to the aircraft. As I walked toward the ramp up to the airplane, a man in an orange shirt patted me on the back while muttering a number as he kept count. Once aboard the cargo plane, they instructed the hundred or more of us to sit on the floor in rows, squished against each other.

Massive straps anchored to the deck stretched over ten of us per strap, like a giant seatbelt. Medical stretchers filled with the injured were stacked three and four high, placed like bunk beds in one of the corners. A small aisle had been created so the military could pass between the rows of people.

Nobody had seen it coming. We had arrived in Haiti the morning of the day the earthquake hit. I looked around and spotted a few of my group members in the crowd of people on the plane. I had just struck up a conversation with a young survivor who sat beside me when I heard someone yell my name.

"Owen!" I looked around for the voice.

Again. "Owen."

I found the voice, settling my eyes on Margaux, who sat a few rows away. My classmate pointed toward two advancing soldiers. Apparently, they had been searching for me. Elijah, another group member, was with them. The plane was too loud for me to yell, so I raised my hand to indicate where I was.

"Come with me." one of them instructed.

I was alarmed, but knowing no better, I obeyed. The young soldier held out his hand to help me up and I took it. He guided me away from where I was sitting. Elijah stayed.

As we walked, I noticed he was holding my arm carefully. With each step I took, he would offer words of encouragement. "Yeah, that's it," and "Watch your step." To him, I was just a kid, but this was way over the top.

I asked what was going on.

"I'm taking you to your mom."

I was even more confused now. Wasn't she with us?

We headed toward the front of the plane where a small fold out of metal stairs touched the pavement. He led the way off the aircraft, offering his hand again for steadiness on the way down. I was deafened by the footsteps of marching troops and the roaring engines of military planes. He let go of my wrist as we walked until we reached an old, isolated city bus. The soldier motioned with his hand for the driver to open the door.

"Get in," he commanded. He stayed on the pavement as the driver shut the doors behind me. Once I saw the doors were sealed, I turned my head to see eight passengers from my volunteer group, including my mom and brother. They looked up at me from their seats, but quickly closed their eyes again. They were getting ready to sleep.

I remained standing at the front, ready to leave, still unsure why they weren't on the plane — why *we* weren't on it. My heart started racing. If we didn't get off the bus immediately, we were going to miss the flight, the flight that would take us home.

"What's going on?" I asked, my voice composed despite my growing fear.

"I couldn't get on the plane," my mom said, her voice surprisingly calm. "So I told the soldiers to go and get you. I didn't want you to leave without me. We have to stick together as a family."

I was pissed. All I wanted was to be home.

"Why couldn't you get on the plane?" I asked.

"'Cause there wasn't enough room," she sat up, continuing. "I pleaded with them to go get you, but they refused until finally Curtis mentioned that you have a disability and then they agreed to go get you."

I glanced over at Curtis, who sat next to his wife Corrine.

There it is. No wonder the soldier was treating me like a kid.

"So they traded Elijah for you."

I gave up, sitting down.

"How long until the next plane?" I knew I wasn't leaving anytime soon.

"I don't know," my mom said. "Hopefully before the next earthquake hits."

* * *

A Few Days Earlier

The morning had come to depart for our trip. Although I was tired, I got up immediately. and walked downstairs, holding the railing for balance as I always did.

Skye and I were born extremely premature at twenty-six weeks. We both came out lucky. However, because of the difficult premature birth, I have three disabilities. Skye is tall at six foot one, where I'm two and a half inches shorter, mostly due to the shortness of my legs. This is caused by a disability called cerebral palsy. My torso tilts forward, almost in preparation for an inevitable fall. Cerebral palsy doesn't get any worse over time and varies from person to person. I have mild CP. It affects my balance and I tend to fall or stumble when my balance is disrupted. I have delayed reflexes, mostly in my legs. I also have a slight limp on my right side and stomp my feet when I walk.

My muscles are tight, especially in my legs. As a result, I'm not flexible so it's difficult to make certain movements. I lack fine motor skills in my hands and even more in my feet.

Skye and I look similar. My face is narrower than my twin's because I spent longer in an incubator so my soft, malleable head formed to be narrower. Other than the height and face differences though, we look identical.

My mom, brother, Skye, and I put on our thick winter coats and hats. We said goodbye to my twelve-year-old sister and a family friend, who was going to be babysitting my dog and my sister, when they weren't at my dad's. My mom drove along the windy, snow covered road before parking at the high school.

Leaving the cold, we entered the Quest room, a room that the school had allowed us to inhabit for the semester. The room was busy but full of excitement — we were going to Haiti! A few people were double checking that they had brought everything, others helped Don, our teacher and founder of Quest, pack bins full of donations; clothes, hats, coloring pencils, and paper.

The two of us had known each person in the Quest group since we had moved from Vancouver seven years ago, other than Jodie and Sage, who were relatively new to the school. Still, we had gotten to know the two of them a lot better since the start of the semester when Quest for Community was formed. Most of them were our good friends. I rummaged through my bag making sure I had remembered everything. Something was missing. Something important. "Hey Mum, you wanna give me a ride back home?"

"Do you need to go back?" she asked. "I'm pretty busy."

"Yeah. It's important."

"Can you ask someone else to give you a ride?"

"How do I put this?" I said. "I forgot to pack underwear."

My mom laughed. "How is that even possible? You and Skye always forget to pack important things. Remember that time Skye forgot to bring pants on our trip to Vancouver?"

I remembered all too well. Skye had entered the car wearing only his underwear, because why not, but forgot to pack any pants for when the ride ended.

My mom continued the story, "When we stopped to get food, he had to wear a poncho. You and Skye are the worst for packing."

"Yeah, I know," I said, looking at her to see if she was going to give me a lift. She went back to packing.

"Hey, Nicole," I said to my classmate standing nearby. "Did you drive today?"

"Yes, I did," Nicole said in an over the top cheery voice, joking around. "Why do you ask?"

"Do you wanna give me a ride home?"

"Of course," She said.

Nicole and I returned from my house to see all eyes watching Don. His name fit his description. He had dark hair that was slicked back and a mustache that was just as dense as his hair, which bounced as he spoke. Quest was made up of seventeen soon-to-be graduates, me being one of them. It was a group focused on volunteering on the weekends, after school, and sometimes during school. So far, we had weeded a community garden, fixed up a daycare, picked up litter along the highway, catered a wedding, picked apples for a spiritual community, and hung out on an indigenous reserve. Haiti was our final project. Where we would build the wall for a goat farm and aid in the funding of a well. But it wasn't just the high school group going.

Sue the secretary (not to be confused with Suzanne, the other secretary at our school) was going to be chaperoning, along with my mom. A local church group was coming as well, although we had nothing to do with them other than going on the same trip. I had only met the church group once before. There was their pastor, an older man named Jim. He wore thick glasses and had a nearly shaved head. The rest of the church group were older, in their mid-thirties, early forties.

"Everyone," Don said, his dense mustache moving as he addressed the class. "When we get to the border, I don't want any joking around. Just hold out your passport and answer any questions they ask. Okay?"

"So..." Skye said, "If they ask about the weed, I'm bringing, what do I tell them?" A few of us snickered as Don scolded him.

The bus was running before any of us got on, something that was always necessary to do before driving in the winter to clear the frost covered windows and to heat the bus.

The last few rows on the bus had already been packed with donation bins. Outside, two of my classmates, Cam and Brooklyn were finishing off their smokes. Cam had short, blond hair while Brooklyn had long, brown hair. With each exhale, smoke came out of their mouths, as well as warm breath that stood out against the cold winter air. The two of them made the cigarettes last because it was something that we were told wouldn't be allowed in Haiti.

I sat down beside Jonathan, a dark haired, half-Quebecois classmate. He was also the only one of us fluent in French, despite the fact that we were going to a French-like speaking country.

6

"I heard they have guys standing on rooftops with guns," Ryan said. "They watch you as you go by."

"That's such bullshit," Skye said. "You just think that 'cause they're poor."

"I don't know," Ryan said.

"Haiti's pretty messed up," Jon said. "Weed is a part of some of their ceremonies."

"I hope we get to smoke weed while we're down there," Kyler, a tall, lanky classmate said.

"Yeah, 'cause they're just gonna bust out a bong in the middle of church." Skye said, before taking a drink of his water. He held it in his mouth, sucking in air, which created a sound that mimicked that of a bong being hit. In the other hand he pretended to hold a light to the end of the imaginary mechanism.

We all laughed. "Owen, would you smoke weed if they offered it?" Cam asked.

"No," I said.

"What if it was super important to the ceremony?" Kyler asked, grinning.

"I don't know. Maybe then," I said.

I had smoked weed before, but not as much as most of the group. I have restricted lung function, my lungs are 75% as efficient as my brother's lungs and the average person's lungs. It's hard for me to get more than a sentence out without taking a moment to breathe, and so I'm a quiet person.

Up until I was three and a half, I had a tracheotomy, a small "smokers" tube that helped me breathe, going from my lungs out my throat, and it's left a sprawl of scars where my neck meets my chest. Because of the scar tissue, my voice is raspy, husky, harsh and very deep.

There wasn't much else to do on the bus other than talk and rest. Don had told us not to bring cellphones or iPods, saying it would distract us from the trip. I didn't care though. I was going on this trip to experience Haiti.

It took a few hours to pass the border and reach our first airport in Spokane. The plane boarded at six p.m. I sat beside Elijah and Sage. Sage, with her light, red hair and freckles, had made it clear the tropics were going to be harsh on her skin. Elijah had long hair, which was filled with beads, matted and wild, much like his personality. If the Quest group had a wildcard, it was him. I got the window seat.

"Hey Owen, can I have that seat if you don't mind?" Sage asked, talking in her usual, fast-paced manner.

"Sure. I don't care," I said.

Some people slept on the plane, but I had never been one to nap while flying or driving. Instead, I read and ate a PB & J sandwich. Two and a half hours later, we arrived in Salt Lake City.

I took off my winter jacket and stuffed it in my bag. Nearby was a luggage measuring device with a sign above it that said, "Check to see if it fits." I shoved my backpack between the metal bars, but it wouldn't budge.

An airport clerk approached. "I'm sorry. It's two inches too big."

"I mean, it fit on the last flight."

"Well, it's too large," she said.

I asked, "Can I not get it on this one?"

"Sorry, Sir," she said. "You'll have to check it." I couldn't help but wonder if I had left my underwear at home then maybe it would have fit.

"Otherwise," she said, "You could try to ask someone from your group to take an item of yours." It was obvious that we were a group of high school kids.

I went up to Aubray and Margaux. Two girls in my class, who always seemed to get their names mixed up, even though they didn't look that similar. Aubray was shorter with long brown hair, and Margaux had bright red cheeks with a matching bright smile.

"Hey, do you guys have any extra room in your bags?"

"No, sorry. Why?" Margaux asked.

"'Cause the person said my bag was two inches too big," I said. "You know me, everything of mine is two inches too big."

They started to laugh. "Oh Owen." I clued in almost immediately, my cheeks growing hot.

"I honestly didn't mean it like that." I said.

"Yeah, sure..." Aubray teased in the way she always did.

"I'm serious!" We all laughed. Nearby, Jonathan loitered, a duffel bag over his shoulder. A duffel bag that could carry more.

"Hey Jon, wanna take my jacket?" I asked. "The airline person told me I needed to clear some room in my bag."

"Sure," he said, opening his bag and stuffing the jacket inside. He struggled with it like a sleeping bag that was too big for its case.

The group and I waited around for a few hours and then caught our next flight to New York. The flight took nearly five hours, but with the three hour time difference, we arrived in New York at six thirty in the morning. Haiti and New York are in the same time zone, and for that reason, we weren't going to be switching times anymore.

We set all our stuff down by some benches. Our flight was at nine a.m. As a result, we had a few hours to kill. Most people tried snoozing on the hard airport floor. I laid down for a bit, but I tossed and turned, giving up shortly afterward. At this point, I figured I would just get some sleep once we got to Haiti.

It was generally pretty quiet, except for the odd whisper or announcements being made over the intercom. I ignored the P.A.

while I read a book. I wouldn't need to start listening to it until we neared the time of our flight anyway.

It was my first time in New York and all I was doing was reading, but I knew I would be back soon. The group planned to stay the night in New York on our way back from Haiti. Our flight was going to be passing through, and Don figured we might as well stay one extra day. I think the general idea was to go on a shopping spree, especially because the closest town to us only had a small mall. In other words New York shopping was going to be amazing. And it was New York! We only had to wait until after Haiti.

Jim was reading the itinerary, holding it close to his thick glasses. The printing on the paper was in big, block letters, abnormally large. I had only met the pastor once before, but it was then that I realized something about him. He wasn't wearing sunglasses or a cane, but Jim was legally blind.

More and more of our group were rising from the airport floor, stretching or yawning, blinking their eyes in a tired motion. Don called us all together, waking me from my book, and some from their slumber.

"Alright guys, grab something to eat before we go. We won't be eating when we land, so it'll be a while until the next time we have food. And change clothes before we leave because once we arrive, there will be no opportunities to change until we get to Haiti Arise." He looked around to see that all of us had caught that. "I'm going to go grab a bite. Does anyone want to come?"

The pastor of the other group stood up and slapped Don on the back enthusiastically. "I will, my good man." Jim said with a big grin. While most disappeared to eat or walk around, I stayed to finish off some cold macaroni I had packed. I was cheap and not willing to spend money on airport food. The three hundred dollars

I had brought was for shopping in New York, with the expectation to spend a few bucks in Haiti.

After finishing my macaroni, I entered the bathroom holding a pair of shorts. All the stalls were full. A man, who had a pair of pants and a long sleeve shirt in his hands, stared at the stalls.

He said something. I looked at him wearing a look of confusion. I wasn't sure if he had been talking to me.

My third and final impairment to finish the trio is my hearing loss. I have decent hearing in quiet environments with little distracting noises. It becomes harder to hear people when they aren't facing me, or they mumble or whisper. Sometimes I don't know who said what, unless I see them say it. I was supposed to be wearing hearing aids, but because looking cool in high school was more important than hearing well, I wasn't. There I was, about to enter a country that spoke a language I didn't know without my hearing aids. But that was the least of my worries.

He repeated himself. "You just coming back? Or going on vacation?"

"Going on." I said.

"Jealous. I'm just getting off mine.

"Right there, he pulled his shorts off and began to slip pants on with ease. I joined, as none of the stalls were opening. After untying my shoes, I took my jeans off. Putting my shorts on was harder and slower, as I had to keep one hand on the stall for balance.

I asked, "Where'd you come from?"

"The Caribbean," he said. "Where you going?"

"Haiti."

"I'm sure it'll be nice and sunny. Anyways have a good trip," he said, leaving the bathroom. I left the bathroom with my shoes still in hand, my socks cleaning the airport floor. I sat down on a nearby bench and put my shoes on, making sure to double-knot them, something I always did.

Eventually, everyone was back and changed. A bunch of us wore tie dyed shirts that we had made in class together. All of them were unique in their own way, only sharing an expression, Quest for Community, in both English and Haitian Creole. The image of two tree-like palms held the world between them. It made us stand out as a group, especially when we were all together.

The only two people missing were Don and Jim.

The intercom started, "Attention passengers boarding Delta Airlines flight 453 to Port au Prince. Your departure time has been changed. Now boarding Gate-" I didn't hear what followed on the announcement. I looked at my boarding pass.

"Was that our flight?" Jodie asked.

"Our flights in an hour," I said.

"Yeah." Rachel, a classmate who had her hair pulled back into a tight ponytail said. She glanced down at her watch. "Our flight isn't for an hour."

"I don't know, was it?" Brooklyn said. There was some urgent chatter as the group shuffled to grab bags. I put my backpack on.

"I just looked at our tickets. That was our flight," Blake, a tall and wide classmate said.

There was a moment of hesitation. Everyone looked at each other, probably all thinking the same thing. What should we do?

"Run!" Someone yelled.

They took off toward the airport gate. I remained with Kyler, Sage, and Sue. I liked to think I was waiting for Sue, who was nearly sixty, but in reality, I knew I couldn't keep up with them. "Where's Don?" Sue asked.

"He's with Jim. I think they're eating somewhere over there," replied Sage. She pointed at a sign.

"I'll go find them!" Kyler sprinted away.

Shit. Are we really going to miss Haiti? After all this?

"We should probably get moving now," Sue suggested.

The three of us started running toward the gate when I tripped over the ground, hitting the hard floor.

"You okay?" Sage and Sue asked in sync. My fall wasn't an unfamiliar sight to them, and it wasn't an unfamiliar occurrence to me.

I was on the ground, but not for long.

"I'm fine," I replied, using my arms to get up. I was always *fine* after a fall. I wasn't going to miss this flight.

Sage, Sue, and I arrived at the boarding terminal to find my mom arguing with an airport clerk.

"I'm not getting on that plane until my son gets here!" She said. As I drew closer my mom pointed at me. "See, there's my son." My mom placed her arm over my shoulders.

"Boarding pass and identification please." I showed her my passport and boarding pass. My mom led me away from her, as if she was our enemy and continued to talk, not seeming to care that the clerk was right there.

"She was telling me I had to board. I told her I wasn't leaving without you."

"Thanks Mum," I said. We watched the side of the airport we had come from in hopes of seeing Kyler, Don and Jim. I didn't think the flight would leave without them, but I didn't know. The woman at the gate didn't seem to want to wait any longer.

Then I saw them. They were running a lot faster than we had been. Kyler lead the three of them, sprinting, his long legs making giant leaps, followed by Don and Jim. When they got to us, each of them was hard panting, frantically searching through their bags.

After a moment, all three followed the rest of us, looking for my seat as I headed toward the back of the plane.

The plane itself wasn't very crowded. It was the emptiest aircraft I had ever been on, many people having entire rows to themselves. I saw the rest of the group sitting at the back, dispersed amongst the seats. I smiled. At the sight of us, they clapped and cheered.

"You guys made it!" Nicole yelled enthusiastically.

We had made it. We had made it to the flight that would take us to Haiti.

2. The Republic of Haiti

The founder of Haiti Arise, the place we were going to stay, had come to our classroom in Canada.

He had exceedingly short hair that barely left his head, and a bright smile. "My name is Marc Honorat," he said, addressing us in our school using his big smile. "And this is my wife, Lisa." The woman was obviously pregnant.

"I am sorry we are late. We had a flat tire," he said. They had driven from a nearby airport. The class was scrambling, the sound of metal scraping against the floor as seats were pulled out filled the room. Within a moment, everyone was staring, watching the foreign couple. "Growing up, my family was very poor. I had fourteen brothers and sisters. My father and mother could not afford me." It seemed like he had told this story many times before, but the emotion in his voice was still raw, as if it happened recently. "I was sold as a *Restavek* when I was five. A *Restavek* is a Haitian child slave. Child slavery is still a big problem in Haiti. I would work all day and was not permitted to go to school. I was only given one meal a day and was often mistreated."

The classroom was quiet, something that didn't happen often. Everyone watched him intently.

"When I was twelve, my older brother rescued me and brought me to Canada. I started kindergarten in Calgary at the age of twelve, graduating from high school when I was twenty five. From there, I went to college where I met my wife. But Haiti has always had a place in my heart. I knew God wanted me to return home. I wanted to create a place for young people to become great, god driven leaders in Haiti. That is when we founded Haiti Arise, a place to educate the people of Haiti."

Marc looked at his wife with a big smile. She took the imaginary mic. "Haitian's take pride in their clothing," Lisa said. "Just because they're poor doesn't mean they don't take pride in their appearance. If you're going to give clothing, make sure it's nice."

"It does not mean you have to go out and buy new clothes," Marc said. "But make sure they are not ripped, torn, or dirty. Haitian's value cleanliness."

"And you too," Lisa said, "must dress nicely while you are down there. In Haiti, for a woman to show her shoulders is like showing her cleavage here. Girls, your shoulders must always be covered. You are to wear dresses, pants or shorts, but nothing too short, and dresses must be worn to church."

I couldn't help but think that maybe this was *their* belief and not all of Haiti. Maybe showing your shoulders wasn't as bad as they were making it out to be.

"Boys," Marc said, "must also cover their shoulders. No muscle shirts or anything that shows your arms. You must be respectful. For the Sunday service, dress pants and shirts are expected."

Marc's wife and kids weren't going to be at Haiti Arise. They were going to be away in Calgary, at their second home, as the two of them were having a baby.

We were in the air just short of four hours. I took out my language sheet and reviewed a bit of Creole. I had two phrases memorized, mainly because they were similar to French. Creole is like French, but mixed with multiple African languages.

The flight attendant handed out papers to fill out for entering the country. The greenslip had an English side and a Creole side. With Jonathan's help, Skye and I tested our Creole skills. We didn't get very far, even while looking at our Creole phrases sheets.

As we drew closer to Haiti, I leaned over to get a good look at the island. Haiti had more vegetation than I had expected, although my expectations weren't high.

I knew that the island had a lot more trees in the past, however, many were chopped down to build houses after the revolution. Haiti was the first independent, slave-revolt nation. But even after gaining their independence from France, they were taxed to poverty by the French and basically banned from trading with most countries for a long time. The nation, despite its strength in revolution, continued to be hindered.

The island was beige, the colour of sand, and the ocean was vast and clear, the kind of clear that sparkled in the sunlight.

The airport, the only one in Haiti, was nothing like any other airport I had been in. It had old tile floors and concrete walls that had been left unpainted. There were no seats for anyone to sit in, and as far as I could tell, only one screen displaying arrivals and another for departures.

A jazz band playing in the corner contrasted the stark atmosphere of the airport. A big banner spread across the back wall in the customs room showed a young Haitian girl, eating some sort of mango flavored product. Some security guards stood in place while the plane was unloaded. The luggage was chucked through a hole in the wall onto a stagnant conveyer belt. There was no air conditioning to subdue the stifling Haitian heat. I definitely didn't need my feathered down winter jacket anymore now that the air around me was warmer than my breath.

Abruptly, Don raised his voice, "Stay together guys!" as I tried to keep up.

Most of us had gone through customs when I heard a yell from behind. "Shit," Sage said, as her hands dug into her bag. "I know I had it here."

"Sage, what's wrong?" Don asked.

"I can't find my greenslip." She began to chuck her clothes in to piles on the floor. "I think I left it on the plane. I don't know what to do." She was speaking faster than she usually did, although she always spoke quickly. "What if I left it on the plane? They'll still let me in, right?" She looked at Don for signs of hope.

Don arrived at the customs desk. "She seems to have left her greenslip on the plane. Is there any way we can go get it? Or do you have other ones here?"

The customs officer looked at them with ease in her eyes.

"It is okay. You can have another one." She handed it to Sage.

"Oh my god, thank you so much," Sage said.

After she filled out her slip, we moved on to the conveyer belt. Four men approached us.

"We work for Haiti Arise. Marc has sent us to collect you," one of them said. We held no sign, but it was obvious that we were the group they were looking for. Everything about us advertised tourists. A couple of the adults exchanged handshakes and words with them.

"Be quick," the chaperone with the hat said as he led us outside to a fenced off pathway. And he meant it. He moved along like we had to get out of there immediately.

On the other side of the fence were dozens of people, each trying to make eye contact and shouting in Creole or broken English. Even if I didn't understand them, it was clear they wanted something. Each man and woman spoke like they had something to offer, like they were helping us, but their pitches rushed as if they needed to convince us right that moment. Hands clambered at the fence, each matched with a smiling, but distressed face.

"They are trying to make a little money by carrying your luggage," said the man wearing sandals, answering any confusion.

At the end of the fence were more people with the same intentions. But this time, they weren't blocked by the fence. Multiple people closed in on us, hands reaching for any bag that looked big, and not hesitating to ask if the tourist wanted their help.

The chaperone with the soccer jersey shouted at the newcomers who backed off.

"Do not let them touch your luggage," he now spoke in English, "unless you want to pay them." He laughed to himself.

The chaperones led us to a group that wore matching red hats and grey pants. "Give your luggage to these men. They will take care of them for you." Each of the chaperones spoke formal English, no slang or contractions.

The uniformed group took the bins and large bags. We continued to follow the chaperone toward a bus and van. One chaperone put his foot on the step of the van, grabbed the rack on the top of the vehicle, and threw his leg up, bringing himself onto the roof with ease. He shouted something in Creole. The other chaperones and the helpers began to toss him up the donation bins. After a moment, they were roping it all down. The rest of the stuff was thrown in the back of the bus or kept on our laps.

A handful of men with light blue helmets with thick block letters reading "U.N." stood nearby a van that had the same lettering. To me, the United Nations presence meant political instability.

19

"Don," I asked, "Why's the U.N. here?"

"I guess you'll have to look into it after this trip," he said with a small smile. It was his way of telling me that I should have studied the country beforehand. He had assured us and many worried parents that Haiti was a stable place to be, and that we had avoided hurricane season. On the other hand, I didn't know much. Sure, I had done a little research. On Halloween, dressed up in our costumes, the class watched *The Serpent and The Rainbow,* a movie about investigating people rising from their graves in Haiti, but I still had no clue what to expect. None of us did.

The group had stopped loading up the van and were now staring at us.

The chaperone with the hat addressed Don, "Give the money to one man. He will split it fairly. If you try and give it out to every man who says he has helped, then you will not be able to know who has helped." "And you will be out of money," the chaperone with the jersey said as he laughed.

The chaperone with the hat said something in Creole. A man stepped forward from the uniformed group. "Give your money to this man," the chaperone said.

Don handed some money to the man who spoke for the uniformed group. Instantly, the man was surrounded by the others in uniforms, each person yelling and gesturing as loud as they could to get some of the money. Some sounded desperate, others sounded angry.

"Hurry up! Get in the van!" the one with the sandals said as he flung the door open. I got in the back of the van next to my mom, Elijah and Kyler. The van was tight and cramped. Four of us were in the back, shoulder to shoulder, and the seats in front of us felt like they were trying to break my knees. I reached over to my shoulder, to realize there was no seatbelts. But at least I got the window seat.

Once we left the airport, we started picking up speed. A lot of speed. Next to us, another vehicle was only a short gap away, matching our speed, despite how close it was to hitting us. The two vans were barely managing not to scrape each other. I was torn between being amused and startled.

"Holy shit," Sage said. "We are so close to the other cars."

From what I saw, lanes were more a suggestion than a rule. The vehicles interweaved like bikes rather than the heavy, over occupied cars that they were. I didn't know where the street signs were. I hadn't seen any, except for stop signs, and even those were limited. As for lighted intersections, they were nonexistent. Even with all the dangers, pedestrians still didn't have the right of way.

Perhaps the most noticeable vehicle that we drove by was a large, vibrant, multi-colored pickup truck and a bus that looked similar. Both were branded with flamboyant colors, Haitian phrases, and graffiti-like paintings of iconic figures. Each was stuffed with people in the back, sitting on benches, standing, or hanging off the side.

Almost all the vehicles on the road were older, from the '80's and '90's by the looks of it. I wouldn't have been surprised if every car in the country surpassed me in age. Lots of busses, trucks, vans, motorbikes, and cars were packed. Nobody drove alone.

I was constantly looking at my surroundings, paying barely any attention to my group in the car.

The majority of structures were made of a mix of concrete and cinder blocks. They were the color of dirt, stained from many years of dirt sneaking into the crevasses, some parts hidden with a layer of vibrant paint over top.

Occasionally, I spotted pots and pans in a small gap between buildings. I got the impression that some people were living there. Later, I learned outside kitchens are a common occurrence in Haiti.

In contrast, we passed the country's large, white Parliament building, which bore the red and blue Haitian flag on top of it. A green fence and gate with large white pillars surrounded the building. It was majestic.

Most people walked around supporting unknown teams or causes, their shirts likely cast aways from some local donation drive back home, a mere memory of a little league second place finish.

A group of children dressed in school uniforms ran along the sidewalk chasing after each other with gleeful smiles. We passed a church with a low ceiling and no doors, instead it was open to the public. In the car there was talk of singing.

"Did you guys hear that?" Sage asked.

"They sound so beautiful," Elijah said. I was tempted to agree and pretend that I had heard it. From all the talk, it sounded like it had been a children's choir.

The city had an opposing image. Port au Prince looked busy; people pushed wheelbarrows packed with supplies, trucks full of people rolled down the street, and transactions happened at every little street vendor. People were busy and moving fast, but still, a lot of people sat around, I could only assume with not much work to do. Haiti was visibly lacking jobs and bleakly poor. Waste littered the streets and sidewalks. As we crossed a bridge, I looked below; piles of garbage sprawled along the creek. The water was brown and murky and there was very little of it. A pig roamed amongst the debris, quick to munch down on any bit of waste, its tail flicking wildly.

Most of us pointed and shouted with excitement at everything that caught our eye.

"Look at that! How does she do that?" Kyler pointed to a woman balancing a large bowl of fruits on her head. He took out a little camera and snapped a photo.

Elijah said, "Dude, so dope!"

I think even if we had had our iPods and phones with us, we would have ignored them. Haiti was dope.

Those of us that brought cameras took photos of our surroundings, peering out the window as the air blew in our faces. I had never been a fan of taking photos, but my mom certainly was. She and her camera convinced me to switch seats, squeezing past each other as the van was moving so the couple could be by the window.

We had had a talk before we left about taking photos of strangers. "Ask them for a photo or wait for them to smile," Don had said. My mom pointed at her camera and pointed to a group of kids who smiled back.

Our van came to a stop due to heavy traffic. Amongst the vehicles were several people carrying milk crates full of items like mangoes or sugarcane.

"Hey, hey you! I want to buy some," Kyler yelled.

The man with the stalks ran over with excitement in his eyes. He said something in Creole.

"I'll take six," Kyler said.

The man offered him a handful of them, much more than six.

"No, no, no," Kyler said. "I'll take a few." Kyler grabbed six. "How much?" The man said something in Creole and then held up three fingers.

Kyler handed the man a few U.S. Dollars. Haitian Gourdes were the currency in Haiti. However, we were told by the founder of Haiti Arise to bring American dollars and then exchange them at the bank once we got there.

The man's smile grew as he took the money.

"Sugarcanes anyone?" Kyler asked as he waved them around excitedly, like a bouquet of flowers after catching them at a wedding.

"Sure, dude." Elijah grabbed one.

"I'll have a taste," Sage said, reaching back.

"Owen? Want one?" Kyler asked. Outside, another man had shown up with a crate full of pop in his arms.

"No, I'm good." I said, but I should have taken the offer—I was already hungry.

"Anyone want pop?" Elijah asked. Nobody wanted any.

"We're good," Kyler said as he shook his head.

We stopped at a gas station to fill up and got out of the van to stretch. An older man neared me, holding out his hand. I knew he wanted money. His feet were covered in blisters and his teeth looked like they were struggling to stay inside of his mouth. He wore dust covered clothes that were torn in many spots.

I looked around. I was tempted to hand the man a few bucks. It was against the rules of Haiti Arise. Marc had told us not to give anyone money. "They will tell others," he had said, "and then others will want money from you."

"I'm sorry," I said to the old man begging, unsure if he understood.

We were back in the van shortly. After driving for a while, we reached the outskirts of Port Au Prince where a large garbage dump was located. Bags and bags of garbage were piled on top of each other, and a small portion of the waste was on fire, exhaling black smoke into the clear sky.

Once outside of the city, the beauty of Haiti's countryside struck me. Everything was so tropical, especially in comparison to the snow covered pine we had left behind. Mangoes and bananas that hung from trees looked ripe for the picking. The plants and bushes were thick and green. In the fields, rows of sugarcane grew up in long stocks that resembled bamboo. Little flocks of animals were everywhere; stray dogs, cows, tied up goats, and free-roaming chickens.

A wall with a gate surrounded many of the houses in the country, I assumed it was a symbol of prestige. Later, I found out different—it was for security. We had been driving for a bit more than two hours when one of the chaperones spoke. "This is Leogane. We are thirty minutes from Grand Goave."

"Did you catch their names?" I asked my mom.

"Yeah, it's Julian. The one driving is Sipap."

Haiti Arise was in Grand Goave. I couldn't wait to see Haiti Arise and help out.

The van made a sharp turn on to a side street. Every moment was now a bumpy one, as we drove down the gravel road. As we drove, a large red iron gate that was joined on both sides by six foot cinder block walls was brought into view. The gates opened at our arrival, revealing a large, rugged yard, littered with mango trees and uncut grass. Following the school bus, we entered the compound, parking beside a lone, white truck. As soon as I got out of the van my knees felt free, no longer pressing against the seat in front of me. Everyone was stretching, feeling the same relief.

"Welcome to Haiti!" Marc said, leaving a conversation with three men. They continued speaking in Creole amongst themselves. "I am so happy you are here! How was the trip?"

"It was great," Don responded. "We're all glad to be here."

"And you did not get a flat tire. That is good," Marc said with a laugh.

After stretching, I looked around. At four acres, Haiti Arise was a lot larger than I expected. Toward the front of the compound was a water tower. It didn't look like your typical metal water tower. Instead, the structure consisted of only concrete, a solid square perched atop a column.

Next to it was the main building, a beige, two story place, with pathways leading inside surrounded by little flowered gardens.

Beside the main building was another building, similar in height and size. Both were two stories tall with beige walls, the doors and window frames painted red like the gate. On the opposite side from the main building was a small, concrete building. In between stood an open field with more tall mango trees and a goat with her kids. The goat was tied to a stick in the ground, the free roaming kids instinctively keeping close to their mother.

We entered the main building as a group. Inside were multiple picnic tables, and a kitchen with an island. Four older women were chopping vegetables and stirring a large pot. I think the first thing each of us noticed was the cooked chicken on the center of the island. The profound smell of the bird made me hungry. It would be a hard wait for supper because, aside from the few who had packed snacks, most of us hadn't eaten since New York. Don had told us to expect only rice and beans, but clearly, he was wrong. And sometimes, it's okay to be wrong, especially when it came to chicken.

"Do not worry, we will be eating very soon," Marc announced as if he knew what we were thinking. "The cooks are just finishing up. Dinner should be ready in an hour." He moved on, all of us following.

"Here is one of the bathrooms. Try to limit your showers." The bathroom was a lot better than I expected. The floors were concrete along with the walls, and the sinks enamel.

"This is the girl's bathroom." Down a hallway were two rooms across from each other.

"This is where the girls will be staying." The girls left us as we made our way toward a red, metal door, almost a miniature version of the gate we had seen entering Haiti Arise. The hinges squealed as Marc opened it, revealing a staircase going up. The stairs were steep and narrow, but most significantly, there was no railing. Going up was never as bad as going down without the stability of a handrail. Out of necessity, I took my time, running my hand along the staircase wall, and met the rest of the boys at the top. By that time, I was panting lightly, and Marc had already showed one of the rooms.

"You can stay in whichever room you like," Marc said. Twelve bunk beds were divided between the two. Each of the beds had a white net canopy, appearing to be made for the children of kings and queens. We all knew it wasn't for the royal treatment, but for protection from the malaria-infected mosquitoes.

At the center of the rooms was a common area with a small variety of armchairs and a woven rug at the center. A stairwell led up to the roof, which cast a ray of sunlight into the room—the only light source. Marc led us to a washroom with standard toilets, showers and sinks. It was a clean, functional room, which lacked any embellishment that we were used to, but it didn't matter.

Marc left while the rest of us went to one of the two rooms to start claiming bunks.

"Bunk beds, eh?" Ryan said. "Never thought I'd be sleeping like Skye and Owen."

"They're the only way to go," Skye said. "Except when Cam used to tell girls that we slept in the same bed."

Cam grinned and said, "Well it's true. A bunk bed is one bed. You guys shared a bed."

"We still do," I said, laughing.

"What do you guys do when you have girls over?" Bryden asked.

"Right," Ryan said. "'Cause they have girls over." The room filled with laughter.

A couple of us changed. I sat down and switched my shoes out for sandals. We had, not long ago, started unpacking when Brooklyn stood at the door. She probably would've come in, but it wasn't allowed.

"Hey guys, Cathy wants to take a group photo of us in front of the bus."

Wow.

We had only been at Haiti Arise for half an hour and my mom already wanted some stupid photo. Skye and I had already been skeptical about her coming on the trip. We just wanted to have fun with our friends without our mom. She always needed to get a photo, even if it was at an annoying time. Whenever Christmas time came around, she needed multiple family photos before we could eat dinner or open presents. And the worst part was, we had to be smiling or she would retake the picture a thousand times until it was perfect.

We went outside. This was one of the reasons Skye and I didn't want my mom to chaperone the trip. We knew she would make us do annoying stuff. We had already gotten photos and had just arrived at Haiti Arise!

"Seriously, Mum! We don't need a photo yet," Skye said.

"Yes, we do. Now go stand by the bus," she said in one of those tones that all mothers have when there's no arguing or reasoning with them.

"Mum, no we don't," I said.

"I can wait here all day," she said. Skye and I knew she wasn't kidding. We were hungry, impatient, and tired, many of us not having slept since we began our journey the day before. Reluctantly, we all lined up in front of the bus, smiled—because we were in Haiti—and let my mom take the picture. We had only been in Haiti a little more than four hours. The bus photo was the only group picture taken in Haiti before the quake hit.

Fifteen minutes after that picture had been taken, at 4:53 p.m., on the 12th of January, 2010, the earthquake struck Haiti.

The Quest Group:

Standing, from left to right: Cam, Katie, Blake, Rachel, Ryan, Bryden, Owen, Jon, Elijah, Skye, Margaux.
Kneeling, from left to right: Kyler, Nicole, Aubray, Brooklyn, Sage, Jodie.

3. The Earthquake

After the photo everyone headed inside, apart from Skye who joined the men Marc had previously been talking with. He planned to pick up some Creole. The adults had decided to stay downstairs while the guys and I went back upstairs and sat in the common area. We settled in, talking and joking. Bryden walked out of the washroom, clothed and drying his hair with a towel before placing a cap on his head.

"How's the water?" Ryan asked.

"It's good. It's warm, and the pressure was alright," our classmate replied. I think we all expected it to be cold.

Suddenly I could hear a rumbling sound. I imagined a large truck driving just outside the building. The noise was confusing. It was everywhere and growing. Our conversation came to a halt.

Instantaneously, the rumbling sound built up with immense power. A chill ran through my body and a knot developed in my stomach — the noise grew louder. All of us were silent. It sounded like hundreds of fists were banging on the other side of the walls.

The floor slid back and forth with incredible force, throwing me to my hands and knees. The building shook violently, doors swung wildly, smashing back and forth. The ground dropped and rebounded, dropped and rebounded. Fear charged through my body.

I may die. And there's nothing I can do to stop it.

I covered my head for protection from falling rubble, but nothing fell. Thoughts flashed, lasting only a fraction of a second. Everything around me was slow and fast all at once, like I was watching it all happen. Every one of my classmates had a look of terror on their faces, a screwed up panic in their eyes.

"Cover your heads!" Ryan shouted.

I have to think.

Briefly, I recalled the memories of living in Vancouver when I was younger. We hid under desks during earthquake drills. There were no desks. We needed something stable.

"Get under the fucking doorway!" Ryan yelled as he hurled himself toward the doorway. He was right. I had been taught doorways were an option.

Run!

Using the stronger of my legs, I pushed off the ground, attempting to make my way toward the door. I was thrown back down immediately with a brutal, unforgiving force. My knees smashed into the floor.

Fuck.

The pain disappeared quicker than I could register it.

There's no point in trying to stand.

Planting my hands on the floor, fully aware of my exposed head if the roof fell, I half crawled, half scrambled as fast as I could in the direction of the doorway. My uncoordinated crawl wasn't stable. I swayed with the ground below me.

As I neared, the building shifted again, jerking me with it. My mouth hit the wall. I reacted, covering my head with my hands, but I needed to keep my elbows on the ground for stability.

All of us tried squishing under the two doorways, but only a few fit. The rest of us remained in the vulnerable outskirts, hoping that nothing would collapse.

The shaking stopped. The noise stopped. My heart pounded and breaths quivered.

As I stared at the floor, I moved my tongue around my mouth to check if there was blood.

None.

Straight away, I looked at the rest of my body to make sure I was okay. A small scratch branched down my bicep. I didn't remember getting it.

We need protection.

There were no desks nearby, but there were beds.

"Let's move to under the beds!" I yelled as loudly as I could.

"No!" Blake said. "They'll break!" I stayed quiet, not wanting to gamble with our lives.

Everyone was panting, hearts pounding, anticipating the aftershock. I assumed there was only so much time until another earthquake hit. The building could collapse.

Breaking the silence, Ryan yelled, "Get the fuck out!"

Elijah bolted, leading the way downstairs. I watched him from the top. When he reached the bottom, he didn't move. He just stood there, paralyzed as he stared at the door ahead of him. A light sound of metal clanking pierced the silence. It was the door latch, still shaking from the earthquake.

"Move out of the way," Ryan said as he pushed Elijah to the side. He tried to open the red metal door, shoving it with the weight of his body.

"It's jammed!" he shouted back as he began to fiddle with the latch. Blake made his way down the stairs, in an attempt to help. The rest of us waited, tense, frozen like Elijah. Ryan's hands were moving quickly, but to no avail. The suspense grew with each moment that passed. Finally, he managed to get the door open. I watched as the rest of my classmates clambered down, skipping steps along the way.

Panting, I stood at the top of the staircase, alone. I looked at the challenge that lay before me.

Shit.

I had never been able to run downstairs without the risk of losing my balance.

If the earth shakes as I'm going down, I'm screwed. But there's no other way off the second floor. I have to do it.

I hesitated for another moment, scared of what could happen, of what had happened. I leaned into the wall for balance, taking the first step. Each step was the biggest and most unknowing step of my life.

I entered the main room, turning my head to search for a doorway. The guys and some of the girls were split between the only doorways. I joined Cam and Jodie under the bathroom doorway.

I looked around, chest heaving, thick panting, waiting for something, waiting to run. Where was everyone?

Have they already gone outside?

Cam and I made eye contact but said nothing. His eyes were silent. A few of the dining room chairs were flipped, and in the kitchen, most cupboards were open, food and cutlery scattered across the floor.

Don and my mom yelled from outside the building, frantically gesturing through the open doors to join them, too afraid to enter.

"Get out! Get out now!" Don yelled, waving one arm violently at us as he did.

"Run! Hurry! Run!" my mom screamed. Her face flared red with a sense of urgency. The gravity of the situation was clear from her expression. I had never seen her like that before.

"Go!" Don shouted. "Get out of there!"

"Don't wait! Just go!" my mom yelled. Cam and Jodie sprinted, followed by others. I stood still, the door to safety a beacon in the distance. It would only take ten seconds to make the run, but the doorway meant protection, running meant vulnerability.

Fuck it. I ran clumsily, my feet picking up speed below me. The moment my feet touched the soil, my mom took my wrist and ran alongside me, away from the building. If she was saying anything, I wasn't taking it in.

"Stay away from the trees!" Marc yelled.

Beneath the trees, mangoes littered the ground. My mom embraced me as we entered the field.

"I won't let you go," she said, uneasily. I could tell she was close to tears simply by the sound of her voice.

I looked around at the group. All of us were in a different shape. Brooklyn and Ryan had started to cry. Others were confused or trying to hold themselves together. My mind instantly went to my twin, Skye. I immediately scanned the area and found him embracing Ryan nearby.

A couple people fell to their knees, hands clasped together in prayer. Some stood observant and in a state of shock. Others paced around in a panic.

I began to reason with myself.

Earthquakes probably happen in Haiti all the time. We've only been here for a short time. It has to be normal.

I thought it was like Indonesia, or any other earthquake heavy place. It had been a big one, I could tell, but I figured we had just experienced an ordinary Haitian earthquake. It just came as a surprise to us because we didn't know Haiti; we had only just arrived, how could we?

I was scared, but tried to think reasonably.

I don't need help. I can handle this myself. I just need to think and remain calm.

"Mum, go hug Skye too," I said, annoyed by the fact that she was comforting me, but not her other son. I was okay.

"Skye is fine. He's hugging Ryan," she said, her voice dry, arms still around me.

I pulled away from my mom's hug. She was overreacting. The entire group was. The disaster was something that happened in Haiti all the time.

"Somebody get this woman some help!" Sage screamed at the top of her lungs. She was kneeling near one of the cooks, an older woman who was clutching her knee.

The injury is probably nothing severe.

Still, I figured I should go look. The panic and chaos going on around me was intense. We had no idea we had just survived the most devastating earthquake to hit Haiti in over two centuries.

"Somebody get this woman some help!" Sage cried out again. I walked closer to get a good look at the cook's knee, only to be flooded with a sense of panic. Her scratched up knee wasn't too bad. That wasn't what scared me. It was the look upon her face. A look that wouldn't be there if the earthquake was an ordinary one. It was a look of pure terror.

I staggered back, hit with the horrific realization.

This is no ordinary thing, this doesn't happen in Haiti often.

I looked around, no longer in a composed manner. I didn't know what to think to calm myself.

What the fuck are we going to do?

Marc had taken out his phone and called his wife.

"Lisa, an earthquake has just hit," he said. "I need you to email the school and the parents. Tell them we are okay but need immediate help." Marc hung up.

Blake yelled, "Where's Rachel?" Nobody responded.

"Where's Rachel?" Blake yelled for his girlfriend again.

Fuck. What if Rachel is gone?

All of us stood motionless, silently watching the building to see if she would emerge. Nothing.

Moments later, a young woman came running out of the building, wearing only a bra and pulling up her jeans, which still hung low on her legs. Clenched in the other hand was a t-shirt. Rachel. Sue followed; her hand clutched at her side as she fled the building. The two of them were still wet from the shower. I hadn't realized I had been holding my breath, but after seeing them I exhaled. Rachel reached the group, wrapping her arms around Blake.

As they made it to the rest of the group, the ground dropped again. I lurched forward, off my feet, hitting the moving ground. Trees swayed viciously, bending so that the leaves nearly brushed the floor. The ground was like a waterbed, its shaking was a ruthless ripple on a hard surface. The buildings before us danced like jello, their walls bending with each vibration.

I curled up and covered my head, scared for my life. Each person was covering their head, and on the ground. A few of the locals yelled and screamed out in Creole.

The shaking stopped. The aftershock hadn't been as strong as the first, but it had brought the same panic with it. Some remained on the ground in fear. Others got up again, moving around, pacing from one spot to another, unsure of where to go or what to do.

After punching some numbers, Marc raised his cell phone to his ear again. "My phone is not working!" he shouted, trying the call again to no success. Perhaps a nearby cell phone tower fell with the aftershock or the lines broke. But it meant one thing, and one thing only, we had no service. No communication.

Marc spoke to Julian, then spoke in English. "A tsunami may come, we must move to higher ground and farther away from the ocean. There is a place about a mile and a half inland called LifeLine. Julian will take you there and I will drive the truck."

"Get in the van," Don ordered. Without hesitation, Quest and my mom began getting into the van. The shaking had stopped, but my thoughts continued.

At the mention of a tsunami, the visual of a mass of water racing, sweeping away everything in its path flooded my imagination. I had never been a good swimmer. Not with my lungs, and certainly not with my cerebral palsy. I wasn't going to make it if a tsunami came, and there was no way I could outrun the earthquake's creation. The next thought crossing my mind brought me a mix of comfort and terror.

A tsunami isn't coming. It's the van that'll hurt us.

I didn't know anything about tsunamis, but I figured two things. The shaking may not be powerful enough to bring a tsunami, and if the wall of water was coming it would have come already, with the initial earthquake or shortly afterwards. I wanted to avoid using the van at all costs. If another earthquake hit while we were all thrown in a van with no seatbelts, getting injured was destined.

Someone yelled, "Owen, get in!" I looked at the vehicle; my mom, my twin, and all my classmates were staring back at me. Everyone was scared and waiting, everyone except me and one other person —Elijah.

What the fuck is he doing?

A broad smile played on Elijah's face as he looked up at the sky through closed eyes. His arms reached up as he rotated his body slowly, allowing his long, bead-filled hair to sway behind him. The wild card appeared to be manifesting to the universe or something.

I hesitated, weighing out our odds. The van was imperfect, but my group was already in it. And maybe they were right. Maybe a tsunami is coming. Either way, it didn't look good, but I couldn't leave them. Especially not my family.

"Get in, now!"

After a moment, I hoisted myself inside, urgently scrambling to find a seat beside Margaux. There were nineteen of us in the van. The wild card would make twenty.

"Guys," I said as loudly as I could, "If another earthquake hits and we're in this van, we're way more likely to get hurt." I looked around for a reaction. Nobody responded. I assumed half of them hadn't heard me, the other half didn't want to hear what I had said. With me inside, all attention turned to Elijah, followed by a bunch of berating.

"Elijah, get the fuck over here!"

"Don't be a dumbass."

"Get in the van now!"

He stopped spinning and paused, still dazed in thoughts, staring at us. Reluctantly, he obeyed, jamming in beside me and sliding the door closed behind him. The driver started up the vehicle as Brooklyn started to cry. Margaux rubbed her back and offered her small words of comfort. Marc had already swung open the red gate, the wall around it was still intact in sections. We drove through, leaving the compound. Leaving the only place we knew in this foreign country.

For a moment, I expected to hear sirens in the distance, instead we were met with cries of agony. The van crawled to avoid colliding with the chunks of rubble covering the road.

Through dusty windows, we saw the havoc the earthquake had brought with it.

People sat outside their recently ruined homes. One stood in patches, allowing us to see that it had lost its entire back wall. The tin roof was slanted toward the missing side, struggling to hold at the front. The other walls had chunks missing and thick cracks that propagated through entire sections. Wreckage covered the floors and ground outside.

Another house had gaping holes in its walls, while the second floor was completely caved in. Only the rebar-laced supporting beams and the fallen slabs remained of the second story. The destruction wasn't the worst part. All I could hear were screams of desperation and pain.

A woman held a baby out toward the van as if she wanted us to take the infant. She was screaming and crying as she held the baby up. Her eyes begged us to take the child and leave her.

A man with wet and wide eyes held another child in his arms. Red blood seeped through the white sheet that was wrapped around the motionless body. I stared at the bloody sheet, unable to react. The girl's eyes remained open. She was dead.

We kept driving through the catastrophe. Blood spilled from a man's head. People were lacerated with wounds. Most people were crying as they sat at the edge of their newly demolished homes. Each set of eyes I met conveyed a story of horror, disbelief, and shock.

Why aren't we stopping?

I think it crossed all our minds, but none of us said or did anything.

We could be helping.

Out of the silence, a voice spoke. "Sage," Margaux's voice was uneasy. "Can you sing something?" Sage began to sing *Three Little Birds* by Bob Marley.

"Don't worry 'bout a thing. 'Cause every little thing, gonna be alright."

The voice of Sage mixed with the brutal and vivid reality of the situation brought tears to my eyes, but I fought them off. I needed to remain calm and strong. We passed more broken homes and displaced people. Other than chaos and Sage's singing, the world was silent. Elijah joined in.

"Smiled with the risin' sun. Three little birds."

I felt unforgiving stares as we passed by, we were the escaping tourists. One man knelt, slapping his hands into the ground in frustration. Hopelessly, a woman rushed toward the van, only to collapse to her knees, shattered. Adults held children close, sobbing as they stood still. Some kids were crying and some kids were silent, staring at us.

"Singin' don't worry, 'bout a thing."

They were more than worried—they were distraught, destroyed. Everything around them was in turmoil. The more brutalities we saw, the more I realized that earthquakes were not something that happened often in Haiti.

"'Cause every little thing gonna be alright."

Nothing was alright. The damage and destruction were endless.

We pulled up to an area surrounded by a chain link fence, with a sign reading *LifeLine*.

4. LifeLine

On foot, we followed Julian into LifeLine.

A battered building with thick cracks that ran through its walls stood at the opposite end of the place. About forty locals sat together in clusters among the grass. Other than the building, people, four lamp posts, and two tables with a twenty liter water jug on each of them, the field was empty. The people weren't touching the water; probably because they knew it had to last them a while.

As we approached, many looked over with distress covering their faces. We sat down, joining them, but nobody exchanged any words. I looked around at the people in the group. Some were sobbing. A couple people held their hands together in prayer. Most were silent. An older man looked at me, mustering up as much of a smile as he could. I smiled back. Then I waited. Waited for nothing and something. Even with nothing happening I could feel my heart and blood still rushing.

My heart went even faster when the ground started shaking. I crouched on the ground, shielding my head out of instinct. It was powerful, like the initial aftershock. A small portion of the locals cried out in terror, while more joined in prayer. I could feel the adrenaline rushing through my body and the fear that followed. I was scared. The earth was vibrating, leaping underneath me, each leap made my heart leap as well. And then it stopped, there was no slowing, it just finished. But the fear remained.

The truck arrived with the church group and Sue, the secretary. Corrine, from the church group, was wearing only a towel, water still dripping from her hair.

I don't know how long we sat amongst the locals, but it probably felt longer than it actually had been. Time seemed to move slowly as we sat around and waited for the next aftershock. They were bound to come again. The ground jumped. I clutched the earth, as it maneuvered beneath me. It was so malleable, so flexible, but was still rock solid underneath my fingers. waiting for it to subside. People yelled in Creole, in fear or in prayer, I could only assume. I couldn't tell the difference. The shaking ceased, but the fear it had instilled in all of us wasn't going to leave anytime soon.

People continued to join the field. Eventually, some people began to stand, knowing the aftershocks were likely to continue for a while, but as soon as a tremor hit, they would fall or sit back on the ground, wait for it to finish, and then return to standing.

We were in a constant state of not trusting the ground, the very ground we had trusted our entire lives. Our definition of normal had disappeared forever. All it took was one moment, and an entire country's faith in its foundation was gone. There was no stopping it or pleading with it. All we could do was sit and wait for it to end. And hope it didn't do more damage than it already had.

People started to stand. I joined them, using my arms to get up. A woman wearing scrubs approached me.

"Excuse me, where's the leader of your group?" I looked around. A lot of people were now in the field. Some people I knew, and a lot of people I didn't know.

"I don't know." I turned to my classmate. "Hey Nicole, you know where Don is?"

She looked around. "No."

"You can tell me what you wanna tell him," I said.

"Okay. I'm a doctor here at LifeLine," she said. "I just got a radio warning from the police. They told me that several prisoners escaped during the earthquake. One of them is known to be dangerous with women. They said he can be identified by a bandage on his left arm," she warned as she touched her arm. Fear rushed over me.

The earth shaking is no longer the only threat.

"Tell the women in your group to stay close."

"Thanks," I said. "I'll let Don know."

I felt a hand on my shoulder. "What's going on?" Don walked up. The doctor introduced herself and began to fill him in on the situation.

"The building is wrecked," she said. "Most of our medical supplies are trapped under the rubble. We're doing the most we can do with what we have, but there isn't much."

"Thank you for letting us know," Don said.

She headed back toward the building. I walked over to the tables with water on them. Beside it was a small stack of plastic cups; I took one and turned on the water, allowing it to fill up about halfway. I could have grabbed more, but I had no clue how long we would be there for. From what I knew, none of the locals had yet to touch it.

"I want us all to group." Don said. Eventually, all of us were following Don, moving away from the Haitians, toward an empty part of the field.

"Why are we moving?" Sage asked. Don gathered all of us at the other end of the field, away from the Haitians.

"Guys, from now on," Don said, "We're going to stay together as a group. I don't want anyone wandering off or leaving this area. I want to be able to see you at all times. If any of you need to go to the washroom, go in pairs or sets, girls and boys. Please, stay safe." He paused. I knew what was coming. "One of the doctors that works here was radioed by the police and told that a man escaped from a nearby prison. He is known to be dangerous around women and can be recognized by a bandage on his arm."

Nobody said anything, but there were small gasps and looks of panic and concern on most of my friends faces.

Don offered some final words of comfort.

"Be careful and look out. Stay strong. You're doing good. I'm proud of all of you. You've been handling this well."

Once Don stopped talking, there was a little more conversation amongst the group.

"How long do you guys think we're gonna be here?" Jon asked.

"A couple days," Cam said.

"A week," Elijah said.

Most of the Quest group thought we would be gone in the next few days. I thought it might be closer to a few weeks. The majority of us seemed fairly calm, still in shock, yet on the edge of panic.

"Don't worry guys, we'll be rescued tomorrow," Sage said in a cheery tone. I could hear the worry underneath it though.

"I want to go home, Don," Ryan said.

"We'll be rescued tomorrow," Sage said, repeating herself in the fast-paced manner she always used. "We don't need to worry." Most of us assumed we weren't going to be leaving the next day. Sage was comforting herself over anyone in a strange cheerful manner.

"Don, I can't stay another day!" Ryan said. "We have to leave by tomorrow."

"We'll see what happens by the morning," Don said.

"Can we drive to the airport tomorrow?" Ryan asked.

I didn't know much, but one thing I was sure of was that we weren't going anywhere, not by the next day. And I think Don was getting that impression as well.

"We'll see," Don said, ending it at that.

A moment passed and the ground shook again. I covered my head. Afraid, all of us clutched the ground. Shouting in Creole filled the air.

Stragglers and groups continued to join the field. Most of those who did go to Lifeline had minor injuries. Limping, clutching their head, carrying children, all of them were being tended to by the few staff at LifeLine.

I had to take a pee so I got some of the guys to go with me. Cam, Ryan, and Skye had to go too.

"It's kinda fucked that we gotta piss in pairs," Skye said as his urine marked the fence. I shivered out of fear. The goose bumps got me thinking about the lack of clothes I had on. The mosquitoes were going to be coming out soon and we weren't covered up.

My mom, Skye, a couple others, and I hadn't taken the malaria shot. We figured we would be sleeping under mosquito-netted beds, which would have been true, but it wasn't —not anymore. I approached Don as I returned to the rest of the group.

"The mosquitoes are coming out soon and most of us are only wearing shorts and t-shirts." Don knew some of us hadn't gotten our shots.

"I'll go ask Marc if there's anything we can do." I watched the two of them speak from where I stood, allowing Don to do the work. After talking, Marc, Jim and Julian drove away with the van. The sunlight began to fade. Another aftershock hit, vibrating the earth beneath our feet, bringing a short lived chaos into the field. I had never imagined an earthquake to have so many aftershocks. It was scary, never knowing when the ground would return to stable.

Nicole asked, breaking my concentration. "Hey Owen, wanna go play with those kids?" I looked over. Nearby were a boy and a girl, aged six and four, sitting side by side.

"Sure." We knew Don didn't want us far away, but we were close to the group. As we drew near, the two kids grew incredibly excited and a woman nearby gave us the biggest smile she could muster.

"Do you two want to play?" Nicole asked. They didn't understand, but we needed no response because it was obvious by their smiles that they liked us. Nicole had always been remarkable with children. For a little while, we just sat.

"What can we even say to them?" I said to Nicole.

"I don't know." She laughed. At first, the boy grasped my hand with his own. We stared at each other, his eyes were innocent and wide, deep and brown. I smiled. I didn't know what to say. He let go of my hand, and raised his own, and slapped it, bringing the lightest of stings.

"What're you doing?" I asked instinctually, fully aware he wouldn't understand. After slapping my hands once more, he pulled his away. I understood. He wanted to play a game of slaps.

We sat across from each other. I placed my hands slightly above his. My palms faced the ground, his, the sky. Since he was the slapper, I had to try to move my hands out of the way swiftly before his hands slapped mine. It was like a game of chicken because, if I flinched, he got a free slap on my hands.

The girl and Nicole were doing something as well, but I was too immersed in my game to pay attention.

He was good, like he had played it a lot before, and my reaction time was slow. He managed to hit me pretty much every time. Whenever he struck me, he would laugh a childish laugh, sometimes he would say something in Creole, and then place his hand over mine again. It didn't hurt and it brought me pleasure to see he was having fun. The amusement of the game kept him occupied.

"Hey guys, who are these two?" Bryden said, sitting down next to us.

Nicole and I looked at each other, each baring the same look of 'I can't believe we didn't ask.' Nicole laughed. "We don't know their names," she said. I hadn't even thought to ask. Bryden and Nicole had taken Russian instead of French in school, therefore I knew it was up to me. I had memorized a little Creole and knew a bit of French and asked them, mixing the two into some broken language.

"*Koman ou rele?*" Neither of them responded. Perhaps I was saying it wrong. "Koman ou rele?" The boy beamed.

"Dieuson," he said. He said it like Di-ew-son. I wasn't sure if that was a name, or a word he was saying. I turned my attention to the girl.

"Koman ou rele?"

She said something, but I didn't catch it. "Did you hear what she said?" I asked Nicole.

"I think she said Kelly." Nicole laid a finger on the girl's chest. "Kelly?"

"Kettly," she repeated.

"Kettly. Okay. And Dieuson," Bryden said.

I poked myself in the chest. "Mon rele Owen. Owen," I repeated, then pointed to my classmates respectably. "Nicole. Bryden."

"*Kel aj a tu?*" I asked. After repeating the question several times, the boy held up all ten fingers.

Wow. I thought, *You're ten?*

I was shocked. The girl held up five digits from one hand and three from another. She was eight, twice the age I thought she had

48

been. Their bodies were evidently small from a childhood of malnourishment.

We switched the game of slaps to a game of knuckles, a game where you hit the other person's knuckles with your own. He became instantly happier whenever he hit me.

Sometimes, the kids would start talking to us, as if because our hands were touching, we could speak the same language.

"Do you know what she's saying, Owen?" Nicole asked.

"No clue," I said. Most of the communication between the five of us wasn't understood. If they said any words, I knew I wasn't hearing them. They spoke their Creole; we spoke our English.

Bryden left. Shortly after, the boy rose, hitting me on the shoulder and then running off, looking back to see if I was following. I smiled but didn't follow. I knew he wanted me to chase him in a game of tag. He returned, hitting me again and then taking off, waiting for a little bit to look back to see if I was following. Once more, I stayed put. I assumed Don wouldn't want me to run off, and I was better at playing other games.

The boy returned, placing his small hands around my arm, and pulling with all his might. I joined him in standing. He laughed.

"*Une moment,*" I said in French, as close as I could get to his language, as I held up a finger. I hurried over to Don.

"Can I play tag with that little kid over there? He really wants to play."

"I'm sorry, Owen. We have to stay close together. It's for the safety of all of us," he said.

"I get it." Although the other adults helped, we were mainly Don's responsibility. He didn't want anything to happen to us.

I returned to the young boy, sitting down and holding out my open hands. His face showed disappointment, but he speedily returned to the laughing boy whenever he hit me.

After a few more minutes, Bryden returned.

"Guys, Marc brought the chicken from Haiti Arise. There's some rice and beans as well." I looked over, and sure enough, he was telling the truth. A freshly cooked, whole chicken sat on a plate, surrounded by a number of other plates of rice and beans. My stomach rumbled. Nicole quickly got up off the ground.

"I'll be back, okay?" She said to the eight-year-old, but got no response. My saliva raced. I remained seated, the boy's hands holding mine. Nicole turned around.

"Aren't you gonna come?"

"No," I said. "I can't eat knowing they aren't gonna."

"Wow," she replied, taking a moment. "That's really good of you, Owen."

"Thanks." I couldn't help but look over at all the food and wish I had taken the opportunity. My mouth filled with so much saliva I was surprised. I swallowed it, temporarily quenching my parched throat.

When Nicole left, the girl had as well, meaning it was just the ten-year-old and I. The boy, probably aware of what I had turned down, squeezed my hand and looked up at me. My stomach still tried to convince me to go eat, but I stuck with the little boy. Seeing the look in his eyes was worth it.

He traced my fingers and right hand with his own. He and I sat in silence for a bit, holding hands. His face was solemn, led by big eyes. I felt a light sting on my hand, and the boy laughed. We returned to our game of slaps.

Soon, dark clouds came over the field, bringing a light drizzle. The rain was welcomed by many, as it meant water. It was followed by a flash of bright light that filled the sky, and moments later, a clap of thunder. A man paced around the field, waving his arms and yelling as if trying to rally people up in prayer or rebellion. Others cried out, their voices floating across the grass, growing with each flash of lightning and subsequent smash of thunder.

The small patter of rain continued, enough to leave a layer of wet along my body.

With the rain came the dark, aside from the little light emitted by the two standing lamp posts, lightning strikes, and the moon. I said goodbye to the boy and headed back to my group. As I sat back down with the Quest group, I couldn't bring my eyes to look at the chicken bones, but I could smell them. A small pile of blankets sat nearby. They hadn't been there the last time I was with the group.

Corrine was now dressed in shorts and a t-shirt. A school bus drove into the field, pulling to a stop near us. Julian stepped out from it.

"You may sleep in the bus if you'd like," Marc said. "It will help with the rain."

A group of Haitians had pitched a tarp up. Others brought blankets, but most remained without anything. A lot of the people in the field were laying down now. We only had a few blankets, so all of us huddled into a small area.

"You two have to sleep by me," my mom said to Skye and I. The three of us laid together on the edge of the large huddle. "The blankets are supposed to be a solution for the mosquitoes." My mom said.

"Hope it works," I said.

Loud enough for the whole group to hear, Rachel asked, "What time do you think it is?" Most guesses were between two and three in the morning.

"It's ten p.m.," Rachel said blandly, clearly unimpressed. There was some groaning throughout the group. None of us wanted to hear that. It felt like days had passed since the earthquake. An extreme number of aftershocks had hit, it felt impossible that it had only been a few hours.

All of us wanted the next day to begin. Nothing would change, but it would mean we had survived the first one.

Aftershocks continued to strike until late into the night. As the evening carried on, the aftershocks tended to be weaker than the first one.

I don't think many slept. I was constantly stirring, trying to find some shut eye. Instead, I found myself listening to nearby conversations to see if I could pick out any of the Creole words. Or I was thinking about what was going to happen. I had no clue on both accounts. Every so often, I forced myself to close my eyes in the subtle hope that I would find some shut eye.

Another aftershock. I remained lying down, letting the earth move my entire body like an over powered massage chair that didn't soothe, but instead, brought a sense of unease and unrest that didn't go away until long after. The man who had been pacing around rallying people was at it again, waving his arms and calling out. Some people in the field yelled in fright. At one point, the rain became quite a bit lighter, the thunder and lightning had finally stopped.

I sat up, observing my surroundings. More people had joined the field. It was hard to say if my group members were asleep or if they were just trying to get there. A minority of the group had moved on to the bus. I decided I would give it a shot.

I sat down a few seats from Blake and Rachel who were cuddled together. I closed my eyes for about five minutes but wasn't feeling it. I wanted to lie down. I wanted it all to be over. Outside, the section of blanket I had been using had disappeared into the huddle.

The night carried on slowly, and the aftershocks continued to be persistent and strong enough to bring fright. I should have felt safe on the ground though, because there were no buildings or trees nearby that could fall on me. But there was still that overwhelming feeling of wanting to run. Quite a bit later in the night Brooklyn spoke, breaking our silence.

"Look!"

Those of us in the field sat up. The Haitians had formed a circle of about two hundred people, all of them holding hands and singing. Previously, I hadn't heard them, but I could hear them now. Maybe I had fallen asleep. The group's singing grew louder. It was full of heart and soul, a gospel like song, filled the field.

"Should we join?" Brooklyn asked.

"I don't know." Nicole said, "It might be their thing."

"I say we do it," Brooklyn answered her own question. As we neared, part of the circle looked back, unlinking their fingers and spreading apart, leaving room for us. Joining them, we filled the gaps in the circle, holding hands with complete strangers. A girl held out her hand for me to take it.

It was the first time any of us had heard Haitian singing up close and personal. I looked around at the hundreds of faces, each person holding hands and wearing a different expression on their face, but each with wide open mouths, singing. We stood for no more than a minute, taking it all in, when the earth moved beneath the circle. The singing stopped immediately.

My body swayed back and forth with the ground, I stumbled but caught myself. The girl next to me squeezed my hand harder. I returned the squeeze. All around the circle I could see people growing tenser, standing against the earthquake. The shaking faded. Nobody had fallen.

Instantly, the singing grew louder than it had before, erupting into the air, covering the field. The gospel filled my ears, leaving me with a warm feeling, that flowed through my body. The foreign language came out of each of them with ease, back by full, passionate lungs. When the song came to an end so did the circle. On one side Kyler let go of my hand. On the other side, the girl let go of my hand. We smiled at each other and then we went back to lying down in the field.

There is a saying in Haiti that goes, *"Ou pa ka manje kalalou ak yon sel dwet,"* which means, "You cannot eat okra with just one finger." It is a Haitian proverb, meaning people must work together.

The Haitian flag bares a similar motto: *"L'Union Fait La Force,"* meaning, "Unity is Strength." Both sayings mean essentially the same thing, one cannot do things alone in times of trouble.

The Haitians in the field helped each other stay standing when the earth shook. We had come to Haiti with the Quest to find a community and that was what we found. It was in Haiti that we witnessed one of the greatest communities ever, but we also witnessed some of the greatest devastation, the sort of devastation that stays with you long after you leave.

5. Haiti Arise

I wasn't sure if I had slept, but I didn't feel tired. I could still feel adrenaline running through my body. I sat up and looked at my body. No mosquito bites could be seen or felt. As far as I knew there had been no mosquitoes at all the night before. A handful of others were already standing, stretching or just staring off into the distance, deep in thought. I looked over to see a dozen people walking our way from the other end of the field. Many of them looked like they weren't from around Haiti. A woman held a small child in her arms. Another woman was trailed by a small toddler. A man with wild, long, brown hair greeted Don.

"I am Patrick," he spoke with some sort of eastern European accent. "Me, my wife, Barbara, and son were staying up at the vacation houses on the mountains near the edge of the water when the earthquake hit. It caused all the vacation houses to collapse, killing some of us. When the houses fell, we came together. I didn't know any of these people beforehand."

Marc had now joined the group to see what all the commotion was about. All of my group was now off the ground, watching and listening intently. "Now, because our vacation homes are gone, we have nowhere to stay. My wife's family lives too far away. We ask you," his eyes pleaded with Don as he spoke, "if we can have a place to stay. My family and all the other people who had been staying up at the houses on the mountain. Please."

"You'll have to ask him," Don said, turning to Marc.

"Yes," Marc said, "You can stay with us. We are about to go back."

"Thank you. Thank you so much."

At that, the group appeared more comfortable, stepping forward and thanking Marc and Don with all the smiles and words they could conjure on their faces.

Don turned to our group.

"We're going back to Haiti Arise now. Anybody who doesn't want to see devastation should get in the truck. Everyone else will be walking back." I wasn't sure where the van was, or the bus. Maybe Marc needed it for something else.

"Jon has no shoes," Skye said. "He should go."

I looked down to see he was right. Jon's feet were bare and covered in dirt.

"Get in the truck," Don said. A few people got in, with Marc in the driver's seat.

I looked around to see if the kids Nicole and I played with were around, but I didn't see them. The field was packed.

We slowly walked back along the same road we had driven on, past many of the same people and homes. Whenever I walk, I keep an eye on the ground to watch out for anything I could trip over. I was constantly maneuvering around pieces of rubble. Sometimes, the rubble was in large chunks, other times the cinder blocks had been crushed down to a semi-fine grain. Pieces of rebar jutted out from the ruins, reaching toward us.

The numerous aftershocks had caused buildings to take a greater beating and left each person with a greater sense of insecurity.

Hour Four

Many of the structures were beyond repair. Tin roofs had collapsed inside of houses that had once shielded them from the rain. Walls that had once offered a safe haven remained standing with little promise of security. Household items and clothing were mixed with the debris found inside many homes.

The survivors we passed sitting on the edge of their broken homes looked on in silence. Many of them shared a hopeless look in their eyes. Nobody knew what was to come, and because of this, nobody wanted to begin the process of rebuilding only to have it torn down again.

We reached the compound. The many aftershocks had done more damage. The six foot wall that surrounded the four acres had mostly fallen, only remaining upright in patches. The large water tower pillar had collapsed, leaving the concrete square containing the water alone on the ground. Luckily, there was no evidence of a leak. However, without the tower, we feared we had no means of getting to the water inside. The main building was in relatively good shape. The building beside it wasn't as lucky.

The front wall of both levels had partially collapsed, resulting in every room being visible, almost like an open dollhouse. From what we could see, tables were turned over, and chairs with missing legs, which had once served to seat students, giving evidence it had been some sort of school. The thing that stuck out the most though was the old-school computers, big square monitors that had been thrown around during the earthquake, smashed and cracked. "The technical school is ruined," Marc said. He counted out loud in Creole as he went over the number of computers that had been broken. The look of distress on his face only increased as the number of items grew.

Major cracks existed on both buildings, but many more on the school. Pieces of wall and roof littered the floors. I continued walking. Beside the school was a wooden church. It looked less like a church and more like something you would see at a summer camp.

The religious structure had no walls. Instead, its tin and wooden roof was held up by thin, wooden poles. Despite its state before the earthquake, it remained unscathed. The only evidence of the quake was on the floor as large chunks of rubble sat dispersed on the holy ground.

Those who had ridden in the truck were sitting on benches that had been pulled out from the church.

"Guys, you gotta try this!" Sage said. A trace of relief could be heard through the stress in their voices. They were speaking of the mound of mangoes that were piled in the center of the benches. Some other men sat on the benches with them eating mangoes. I recognized them, they had been talking with Marc when we arrived.

Enthusiastically, all of us grabbed one and sat down on the benches. My hands scrambled to peel it as fast as possible. My stomach was burning with the hunger. It felt like so long ago. I took a bite and was filled with a magnificent, juicy feeling.

My hunger only increased as I ate, as if my body had forgotten the friendly familiarity of food. I ripped off every last bit of mango from its skin, allowing slits of mango to rest in between my teeth. I picked those out and ate them, too. Hurriedly, I finished it off, at which point my face and hands were covered in mango juice. I held my hands up and allowed the juice to run from my hands to my mouth.

I looked at the pile of mangoes hungrily, wanting more. There were a lot, but there was no other food around. Cautiously, I decided to consume just the one, in fear of tomorrow's hunger. At that point, it looked like everybody knew we weren't leaving anytime soon.

Marc was still walking around. He ran over to the small building on the other side of the compound and disappeared inside. After a few moments he emerged.

"The generator is working!" Marc said. *A generator*? I was surprised they had one.

As we sat on the benches, a few of us talked about the only thing that we could possibly think of.

"I wanna do something, I mean like help," Nicole said.

"Yeah, me too."

We asked Don, "How can we help?"

"I don't know." He took a moment. "I'm glad you guys want to help, but I don't know what we can do." We walked up to Marc.

"Marc, these guys want to help. What can they do?" Don asked.

"We are about to retrieve things from the building," Marc said. "You can help carry them. I have already been inside. The safe was broken into. The ten thousand dollars is gone."

Shit. That was the money we had raised to drill a well for a nearby village.

"I'm so sorry," Don said. A sense of hopelessness had filled the air.

Everyone made their way toward the building. I followed my mom but spoke up before it was too late.

"Hey, Mum," I felt guilt growing inside me, like I wasn't doing my part, "Do you think anyone would care if I stayed out here? You know, like if another aftershock hits, I'm-"

"I think that's a good idea. I'll make sure to look for your stuff." I was thankful of her response. I didn't want to enter the building again, my disability certainly didn't want me to.

"You don't need to," I said. "It's upstairs."

"I'll try my best to find it," she said.

"Thanks, Mum."

Much of the Quest group, along with some locals, started to grab things from the main building. They brought out anything they could find, leaving it just outside the front doors. Each of them was rushed, running in and out, careful of what could happen.

I brought the items from the doorway to the wooden church. *I wish I could do more to help*. I felt practically useless.

Marc and a few men entered the building together and after a few moments, I could see two of them inching backwards, struggling with the weight of the stove in their arms. Marc and the other man held it on the other side. Marc shouted what I could only assume were instructions for getting it out of the building.

Each twist of the cooking appliance brought them one bit closer, and yet somehow one bit farther to getting passed the door. With one last lurch, the men succeeded, continuing to lug it toward the middle of the field where they set it down. They returned to the building, grabbing anything that could be used with the appliance: pastas, rice, and other types of canned foods, mostly beans. It seemed like most, or all, of the food had to be cooked.

From there, Marc walked over to a concrete block on the ground. On the side of it was a lever. "There is still water in the well that we can use," he said. "We must use it sparingly, for the water tower will not work. If you need to go to the bathroom, there is an outhouse in the back." I hadn't seen the outhouse or the well before but was happy to hear they existed.

Before there had been four cooks, and now there was one. The other three must have gone home to their families. The remaining cook began to prepare pasta in a large metal pot.

Once the pasta was ready, the generator was turned off. Its power had to be conserved. The pasta was placed on one of two makeshift tables, which had been made by pushing together two benches and placing a piece of drywall over the top.

We lined up, dishing out food onto plates that had been taken from the building. I reached the cook at the end of the table.

"*Mesi. Koman ou rele*?" A big beaming smile lit up her face.

"Lucianna-" she said, followed by a bunch of stuff I didn't understand.

"I'm sorry I don't know what you said." I said, fully aware she may not understand.

"She said she appreciates it." A little girl, no older than thirteen beside her said. "I am her daughter, Ludcie."

"Nice to meet you." I said.

On the table, next to the food was salt, pepper, and a big bottle of hot sauce. Back home, Skye and I would add excessive hot sauce as a competition to see which twin could handle it better.

Bryden, Ryan, Skye and I poured it on, the red sauce spreading over the pasta like a parasite. After taking a few bites, I was hit with overwhelming spice. Tears formed in my eyes. Every few seconds I hiccupped. I had built up a pant. My nose ran steadily. At the same time my stomach growled, wanting more. My tongue swelled.

I tried to say that I regretted putting on the hot sauce, nothing more than a slur was heard. The others looked at me with teary eyes, each of their faces growing red, receiving the same fiery treatment. It was too hot to eat, but we had to keep going—we were hungry. None of us were willing to let it go to waste. We couldn't afford to.

After lunch, Marc left. We did nothing the day following the earthquake other than some dishes. None of us knew what to do. There was a lot of sitting around, unsure of how to help out. What if people came to rescue us and we were gone? None of us took any projects into our own hands, something that still fills me with guilt today. We didn't talk much either; there wasn't anything to talk about other than the things we didn't want to talk about.

Marc returned as it got later. "I received some unfortunate news when I was gone," he said, holding himself together. "Two of my nephews have died during the earthquake."

"I am sorry for your loss." Don said, everyone else offered him words of comfort.

I couldn't imagine what he was going through. He had lost his nephews, his country was in turmoil, his compound and life's work were in ruins, and he was still putting us before himself.

More people were showing up, walking into Haiti Arise, over the broken wall and searching for Marc. A mother held a small infant and lead a group of three small children into the compound, looking around before setting her pace toward Marc. I couldn't hear what they were saying, but a few moments later, she walked toward the wooden church, settling down on a bench.

Marc and others dragged air mattresses from the main building to underneath the wooden church. Additionally, they pulled out various blankets, most being thin sheets.

Originally, the rules at Haiti Arise were that girls and guys couldn't sleep in the same bed, seeing that they were religious and all. But our teacher had another suggestion.

Don said, "Those of you that are comfortable with the idea should sleep one girl and one guy to each bed. That way, it'll be easier to fit on the mattresses." The thought process worked pretty well, because there were nine guys and eight girls. The Quest group started pairing up, it was like a school assignment, the project -to share a bed.

"Wanna just sleep together?" Skye asked me.

"Sure, I'm down," I said. We had shared smaller spaces. I guess Ryan had been right, we would have no girls in our bed.

It was silent other than the chirping of crickets. As we lay ready to fall asleep, Rachel spoke up, loud enough for everyone to hear. "What time do you think it is?" People made their guesses, averaging around ten p.m. We all remembered what time it had been the day before when she had asked the same question.

"It's six thirty." We laughed. I was surprised, but the more I thought about it, the more it made sense. Back home, during the wintertime, the sun fell around six thirty p.m., usually even earlier. We associated the sun and warmth of Haiti with Canadian summers, when the sun fell at nine or ten at night. And it felt like summer to us, but it was still winter to the Haitians.

I got up to take a piss, walking over to the forest. It came out a dark yellow. When I returned to Skye, I fell asleep immediately. I usually slept like a rock, but not that night because even the rocks in Haiti weren't stable.

6. Two Stories

I woke to the bed moving and the ground shaking. Immediately, pushing myself up with my arms, I ran away from the wooden church, fearful of its collapse. Everyone was faster than me, but I didn't have far to go. I got to the field, panting lightly, half out of fear, the other half out of necessity. I remained standing because the aftershock wasn't strong enough to knock me over.

While some of the locals were clutching the ground, others had stood up, yelling in Creole and raising their hands to the dark sky.

I watched the wooden church, to see if it would fall, but it made no motion of the sort. The mother and children had not moved from inside the church. They remained, clutching the ground, barely covering their heads with small hands. The mother wrapped her arms and body around the baby, shielding them, leaving herself vulnerable.

The first of the group went back, the rest of us reluctantly followed. Skye and I laid back down. I wasn't too sure about sleeping under the wooden church, but I knew it would shelter us from the rain if it came, and at least we weren't in the main building. I didn't know this until later, but the main building was the only building with two stories that remained standing and stable in the entire town of Grand Goave.

We got up early and had breakfast sometime later. The food was decent, but there wasn't much of it.

A few people went inside the main building to grab things. Still, I remained outside, cautious that my disability would make it difficult for me to escape the building if anything went wrong. Some of the items that came out of the building included probiotics and vitamins (which my mom handed out to all of us), a soccer ball, a deck of cards, journals, chairs, blankets, and seasoning for food.

Bryden, Don, Jodie, Katie, Kyler, and my mom found their cameras. Each of them went around taking photos of the compound that day. There is a gap of photos between the bus photo and our third day in Haiti.

Most significantly, someone found a first aid kit. Ryan offered to dress the injuries; he had worked as a lifeguard the summer before and on weekends during school.

We walked toward Don and Marc.

"We wanna help," Nicole said.

"We're tired of sitting around doing nothing," Brooklyn said.

"I want you guys to help out. I really do," Don said, "But I don't want any of you to leave the compound." I understood. Don wanted to keep us safe. To him, outside the compound was the unknown.

"How about you clear that road of rubble," Marc suggested, pointing to a narrow road that ran beside the compound.

We walked toward the wall, passing a goat and her kids as we did. The mother goat made a noise.

Skye said, "The goat sounds like it's saying your name, Cam."

"Yeah, it sorta does," Cam said, grinning.

Skye bleated, "Caaaamm." A bunch of us laughed. "Caaam. Caaaam" Others joined in, attempting to mock the goat, making their voices sound shrill.

"Caaamm. Caaammm."

Cam laughed. I didn't bother joining in, I knew I couldn't make my voice go that high.

The road was covered in rubble, most of it from the wall of Haiti Arise. Each of us stepped over what remained of the wall with ease. I bent over, grabbing a chunk of rubble so large my hand could barely grip the concrete, and chucked it over the wall into the field of Haiti Arise. Another person threw a piece of debris, it bounced, landing near a kid goat.

"I swear if any of you hit them, I will kill you," a voice said, followed by laughter. I remained looking at the ground, grabbing another piece of rubble, and throwing it into the field. After some time, the road was cleared, and we walked back over the broken wall, re-entering our safe haven.

Skye and I were just back when a young man spoke up.

"Are you two twins?" he asked. He had short hair, was thin, and I could only assume he was about our age.

"Yeah," Skye replied.

"Come with me," he said, leading the way. We followed with no hesitation. He took us over to a young woman who also appeared to be our age, maybe a couple years older. She had a few scratches on her face and her leg was dressed in a large bandage. He sat down in one of five available lawn chairs, making a gesture for us to join.

"Are you guys twins?" Skye asked as he sat down.

"No," the girl spoke. "I thought it was interesting that you were." I sat down.

"Your English is good," Skye said.

"We came to school here. We know Marc well." Abruptly, she continued, "My name is Flore and he is Stevenson."

"I'm Skye."

"And I'm Owen."

"Who is older?" Stevenson asked.

"I am," said Skye, proudly.

"I would have thought that you were older," Stevenson said addressing me. I wasn't sure whether that was a good or bad thing. Perhaps he thought that because of my voice.

"How much older?" Flore asked.

"Fourteen minutes." Normally he would joke about having fourteen more minutes of life experience, but this time he didn't.

"I always wished I had a twin. I have a brother." There was a small silence as all of us watched Flore, who eventually continued, her voice growing distressed. "I was in Port au Prince when the ground shook. My house collapsed. The roof fell right on top of me." The result was visible from where I sat. She continued.

"I tried to escape, but I could not. The roof on top of me was heavy. Very heavy. I called out for help and God heard me. I was very lucky because my brother came to check on the house. He helped dig me out from the rubble. From there I walked here. It took me all night to walk from Port Au Prince to Grand Goave.

"Port Au Prince is much worse than here. The buildings are much bigger in the city. There is more to fall. The streets have many bodies on them. People are walking around with masks on and toothpaste under their noses to cover up the stench of the bodies. I do not know how many people have died, but it looks like a lot."

There was a long silence. I didn't know what to say. Nothing could bring comfort to the situation. After a while she changed the conversation, turning her head toward me.

"Can you sing something for me?" She looked straight into my eyes. "Both of you," She said as she looked at my brother.

"Uhh… We can't sing," I said.

"What?" Flore questioned me in disbelief. "Everybody can sing."

"Yeah, I'm sure everyone here can," Skye said. "But we haven't practiced."

"Why not?"

"Nobody sings in Canada," he answered.

"Everybody in Haiti sings." Flore said with a big smile, "And everybody can sing. All you have to do is try."

Skye and I looked at each other, considering the options.

"I don't know," I said. I had never been good at knowing lyrics to songs because of my hearing loss.

"Come on, do it," She said.

"Alright, I guess," Skye said. "What do you want us to sing?"

"Whatever song you want to."

"I only know two songs. The Canadian Anthem and Happy Birthday," I said.

"Pick one then!" she said.

"Wanna do Happy Birthday?" I asked.

"Yeah. It'd be easier than Oh Canada," Skye said, grinning.

We stood up and sang.

"Happy Birthday to you." I took a breath. "Happy Birthday to you-" From where we stood I could see that some of the Quest group watched. The two locals laughed, full of heart, as tears entered both of their eyes. Stevenson banged the chair with his hands. We sat down with grins on our faces. Both of us knew it had been a show for them.

"Okay, you proved your point. You cannot sing," Stevenson said.

"Hey." Flore hit him. "No, they were good!" she said, "You should sing for our friends sometime." She pointed over toward a group of people sitting beneath a tarp.

"Not gonna happen," Skye said, shaking his head.

"Yeah, sorry," I replied unapologetically. They laughed.

"It is okay," Flore said. There was a small silence, but Flore was quick to capitalize. "It was too cold last night. I was shivering."

"What?" Skye said.

"Are you serious?" I asked.

"Yes. You are not cold?"

Skye and I began to laugh.

"You don't know what cold is," I said.

"Winter doesn't even exist here. My back is covered in sweat," Skye stated.

"Our sheet is drenched when we wake up," I said.

"It's frickin' hot at night," Skye continued.

Stevenson looked at Flore to see if she believed us. Both wore the same look of disbelief. We laughed some more.

"Wow," Flore said, "Where you two come from it is colder than here at night?"

"Way colder," I said.

"Have you ever seen snow?" Skye asked.

"No," Stevenson said.

"It's like rain," Skye said, "but colder."

"And it kind of looks like sand," I said. "Wow," Stevenson said. "Very strange."

"It was nice talking to you, but I think I will go back to my friends now," Flore said. "We will speak with you later." It came out of nowhere, but we accepted it. She obviously had a lot going on.

"Sure. See ya later," Skye said.

Skye and I rejoined the Quest group. In another set of lawn chairs were a couple of U.N. workers along with a few locals and Marc. Together, they were listening to a radio which crackled out Creole. I was tempted to go ask them if they had any information but made the assumption that whatever knowledge was shared would eventually be passed down. Each of them were listening attentively yet overtop the announcements, they spoke to each other. A few minutes later the people with the blue berets got up, taking their communication system with them.

Near the middle of the day, Skye and I were talking to Stevenson when lunch was called. Quest walked toward the serving area. Skye and I stood up, ready to eat.

"Aren't you coming?" Skye asked Stevenson.

"Your group is going to eat. You should go with them," he said.

"Come with us," Skye suggested.

"No. You go first," he said.

"Just come with us, man," Skye insisted. Skye and I looked around at the group. None of them were moving.

"I am not allowed to eat when you eat," Stevenson said.

"What?" Skye asked.

"I am not allowed to eat before you. I must wait for your group to finish. Now go eat," he said, gesturing toward the food table.

"Why?" I asked.

"Because I am not allowed," he repeated, his voice on the verge of anger. "We must wait for your group to finish eating before we can have our plate."

His tone changed back to friendly. "Now go eat my friends, before there is none left."

We looked around at the others who stared up at us from where they were sitting. Each face was solemn, fixed in its way, unvarying as they stared back at us. With reluctance, and an exchanged look, the two of us decided to listen to him. We moved away from them toward the food table.

We sat down with some of our classmates. "Bryden had a lot of food on his plate today," Rachel said.

"Yeah, I saw Corrine and Curtis with a lot on theirs, too."

We were all hungry. Every bit mattered. "I even saw them throw some out afterwards."

"It's worse for the Haitians though." Skye told them what happened with Stevenson. "He said they had to wait for us to be served."

"That's bullshit."

"Yeah, I feel bad," Skye said.

"I'll go get Don," Nicole said. Don came over and we told him the situation.

"I was unaware of this. I'll go ask Marc what's going on." Don returned after a few moments.

"We're eating first because if they do, they'll take as much as they can. If they aren't held within limits, they'll take a lot more food on their plate," he said. "I know it doesn't seem fair, but Marc has a point."

"They're nice people, though," Brooklyn said.

"I'm sure they're all good people, but in times like these, people take what they can."

I looked over at the food table to see Lucianna dishing out portions to a line of people. The locals didn't even get to serve their own food.

I have to be more cautious about how much food I take, more cautious than I have been. Don continued, "I have more bad news. We're going to need to start rationing more than we have been. Instead of three meals a day we can only have two, which is the standard in Haiti, and they'll be significantly smaller. Be aware of how much you are taking because if we take it all then the Haitians will have none." We didn't argue with him.

Barbara, Patrick, and the other vacationers were getting more comfortable. The girls had given Patrick the nickname "Tarzan" because he sort of looked like him with his long, dark brown hair and toned body. It didn't help that he walked around in a cheetah spotted speedo at the time.

I didn't get to know much of the other group too well, I just knew there were twelve of them: Barbara, Patrick and their baby; two women from Chile; two older men; an older and a younger woman; and Steve and Laura with a child.

A group of us sat around exchanging stories. Sue spoke up. "Rachel and I were in the bathroom when it hit." Sue was saying *it* not the earthquake, I thought. Perhaps she didn't want to remind herself of what it was, what it had done. "I had just gotten out of the shower when it happened. A large mirror fell from the wall and landed on top of me. I couldn't get up. It was too heavy. Rachel stayed behind to help me." The old secretary looked over at Rachel. "She lifted the mirror from on top of me and helped me get up from the floor. I am so thankful for what she did. She saved me."

That was why Rachel had been late. She had saved Sue, risking her own life.

From the group of vacationers, two older men shared their stories of loss with a couple people from our group. They spoke for one another.

"He lost his wife," one of the men said, pointing to the man who sat beside him. "He was holding her hand as they were running out of the building and then the building fell on top of her. Her hand was taken right out of his." While this took place, the other man stared at his feet in silence.

It wasn't until then that I realized why they spoke for each other. Because otherwise they would have broken into tears.

The man who had been quietly staring at his own feet spoke with an uneasy voice, pointing to the man who had just spoken for him.

"He lost his six-year-old son."

7. The Goat Farm

While some socialized with Barbara, Patrick and the other vacationers, others wrote in their journals, played cards, or walked around snapping photos of the compound. Underneath a tree, some of the children staying at Haiti Arise held a long, metal pole. They struggled with the weight of it as a few of them lifted it, the pole swinging with unease as they attempted to knock down the highest of the mangoes. Jonathan and Skye joined them, grabbing the pole and jabbing at the fruit, causing them to crash to the surface. The children took most of them, but Jon and Skye didn't come without a price. The two of them returned using their shirts to create a makeshift bowl full of mangoes.

I didn't want to take away mangoes from the locals, knowing they would probably need them. Instead, I decided to walk around the compound to get a good look. A small forest grew toward the back of the compound, it was filled with mango, banana and other sorts of trees, bushes, and tall grass. Crickets and other bugs crawled and jumped around.

I had never seen a banana tree before. I had always imagined that the bunch of bananas pointed downward, but was surprised to see that the bottom actually pointed upwards. The fruit was still quite green and small, making them inedible. Before leaving the forest I took a piss, the colour a dark yellow.

Don had been encouraging us to drink water so we wouldn't get dehydrated or get heat stroke. I knew he was right, but tried my best not to follow his advice, knowing the people at Haiti Arise would need it far beyond our stay. Our presence would have an impact longer than we were there.

After checking out the back, I returned to see Cam, Katie, Nicole, Margaux, and Ryan playing soccer with some little kids. The kids were nimble. Even the youngest of them maneuvered their small feet around the ball with relative ease. They were all laughing, having fun. Part of me wanted to join, but I felt like I would be holding back the game. Any of the kids could have beaten me.

Instead, I grabbed a pencil and a few pieces of paper and wrote down some of what had happened. I wrote about Lifeline, and about Haiti Arise. It didn't occur to me until later that I never wrote about the earthquake. I looked up to see my mom standing nearby with a newborn in her arms. It was the baby that was staying with the family underneath the church. I put the pencil down.

"Hey," I said, looking down at the baby. The newborn's fingers were wrapped around my mom's one finger as it sucked on it. It was clearly trying to get food the only way it knew how. My mom was rocking her body slowly, letting her knees bend and straighten slightly as she did.

"Hi," she said. "You know, at most, this baby is a few weeks old."

"Wow, really?"

"Yeah, and her mother's been gone all day. This newborn baby was left with her siblings. She hasn't eaten all day. I let her suckle some food I chewed down to a paste off my finger, and her mother must've breastfed her before she left, but that's not enough. This baby's starving."

It wasn't until then that I truly looked at the baby's face. Her eyes looked sunken into their sockets, with bags underneath them. The chubby cheeks so often associated with babies were barely visible.

"Shit. What're you gonna do?" I asked.

"Well, just keep feeding her a little bit of paste. The baby needs her mother." I didn't know what to say, but my mom did. "Only a mother can do a mother's job." That night, the adults of our group held a meeting to talk about getting out of Haiti. Anyone was free to join they informed us. Sage was the only one to participate.

What I had failed to notice was that Jim had been gone all day. Jim, following a local man, entered the compound.

"I've been looking for internet all day in the hopes to contact home," he said. "No luck so far."

While most of us were lying down in bed talking with one another, a young man about our age came toward our sleeping set up.

"Hi, may I talk with you?" he asked.

"Yeah dude, feel free to join. I'm Ryan," Ryan said, holding out his hand to the newcomer.

"I am Richardson," he spoke a little nervously. On his head he wore a bandana.

"Did you go to Haiti Arise?" Katie asked.

"Yes. I took English, Bible studies, and many other courses here. I am the cook's son."

"Lucianna?" Katie asked. She laid in the bed beside Skye and I. "Yes!"

"She's the best!" Katie said. "And your sister is Ludcie?"

"Yes, my sister is Ludcie." He said. "I have a brother named John as well." He readily became more comfortable, sitting down next to Ryan and Aubray.

"Tell us about Haiti." Aubray asked.

"We are poor." He said, "And the earthquake has ruined everything. My uncle has died during the earthquake, and they have done nothing to help the people of Haiti!" Richardson raised his voice, on the verge of tears. "The government is gone! I have heard many of its buildings are gone and many of its people have died. Haiti is without a government." He glanced over at the sleeping children and their mother, lowering his voice down to a whisper. I only caught snippets of what he was saying.

Richardson stayed with us for an hour, describing what living in Haiti was like, especially after the earthquake.

Skye and I laid down to find our air mattress had lost a lot of air. Most of the air stayed on my side because Skye was heavier than me, causing me to bounce at even the lightest movement from Skye's side of the mattress.

"You know," Katie said, "if an aftershock hits tonight, I'm gonna hide under one of these benches." She began to squeeze herself underneath a bench. "I think it'd be safer than running."

"Maybe," Nicole said. "It sounds like a good idea. I'm going to run though."

Both options would take time. Time we might not have. Skye said to me, "You know how I was trying to catch the language off of those local guys?"

"The ones Marc was talking to?"

"Yeah," he nodded. "I was the only one in our group who was outside when *it* hit. I wasn't sure if you guys had made it until I saw Marc come running out of the building. Before that, I wasn't sure if you guys had survived. It was scary. I was scared for all of you."

Shit. I hadn't thought of that.

"Fuck." I had experienced that same feeling, but with Rachel, not the entire group. "That must've been intense."

He nodded, keeping his cool as he offered his best smile. "It was."

We fell asleep shortly afterwards.

It didn't matter what I dreamt of, where my mind would take me when I slept, I always woke to the same reality. To the ground shaking below me. I jerked up, pushed myself up with my arms, and ran as fast as my body would allow away from the shelter. I joined the Quest group, aside from Katie who hid under a bench. The shaking stopped, but my breathing had not.

"Hey guys," Margaux said. "I was awake when the ground started shaking. The crickets stopped chirping a moment before it happened. They know when it's coming. If you hear them go quiet, run." I couldn't hear them.

What Rachel said next brought shivers down my back. It was the same reason, after Haiti, many of us roused at the same time each night.

"It's four in the morning right now. Every night around four there's been an aftershock."

On the fourth day, I awoke to the earth trembling. Immediately, I was up and out of bed. The shaking had subsided before I had even made it out to the field.

That was over quickly. Almost too quickly.

I turned around to see Skye, crouched over and backing away from our bed. He had been pushing down on the air mattress to make it seem like an earthquake. Skye joined Cam, Jon, and Ryan who were laughing hysterically. Jon patted him on the back. A few others joined in on the laughter.

"Holy shit, that was funny," Cam said.

I rushed over toward Skye, my adrenaline pumping.

"Fuck you," I said. And then a moment later, adrenaline still pumping, I grinned. "It was a good one though." I had to give him that.

"Sorry, bro. I had to do it." He opened his arms. I moved in closer and wrapped my arms around his back.

"It's cool," I said, turning my attention to Jon. "Happy Birthday, dude."

"Thanks, man," Jon said. He was the first of us to turn eighteen. The first of us to become an official adult.

My mom was already up, rocking the starving baby in her hands. A bowl of milk sat on a bench nearby. The mother was nowhere to be seen.

Over the days, leaving in the morning and returning at night had become the mother's routine, leaving her baby's fate in her siblings and the few hands that cared. I assumed she had things to do, to help her family, but still, it was a ruthless reality, whatever the mother did would never be enough. Some of the boys were still laughing when Marc came up to us, "If you would like, you can move the wood from the back of the compound to the middle of the compound, by the stove. It will be harder to loot that way."

"We can hand out the donations to the kids while you do that," Sue said. The secretary and a couple others started taking lids off of the donation bins.

A group of us followed Marc along a path through the back of the semi-forest.

We reached a concrete structure that had once sheltered a lot of wood. It still sheltered the wood, but one of its three large concrete pillars had fallen, covering the wood with chunks of rubble. The tin roof remained standing, even with the fallen pillar. The wood looked like it had been previously stacked but was sprawled out from the earthquake and aftershocks. The wall around the back of the compound was mostly gone. A variety of kids climbed on it, seeing who could make it to the top, making a game of the broken wall. At the sight of us, some of them waved excitedly and smiled big playful grins while a couple of the younger ones ran, too shy to interact.

There was a decent amount of wood, but it was light, so we moved swiftly. Some of the little kids who had been playing on the wall offered to help as well. One of them had an eye that was half closed, although I assumed it had been that way before the earthquake because it wasn't swollen.

I tripped over my own feet and plummeted to the ground, throwing the plank of wood ahead of me, bringing up dust as it landed.

"You alright?" Skye asked.

"Yeah."

He always knew I was *alright*, but never refrained from asking. And he always offered me a hand up. I never took it, though. I didn't need help. I was fine by myself. I got myself off the ground and then looked down at my knee. *It's fine.* I would have left it alone, but Aubray spoke up.

"Owen, you might want to get Ryan to clean that up."

"No, I'm fine," I said. "Happens to me all the time." A couple layers of skin had been torn off, but it wasn't bleeding. "We're in a foreign environment. It may get infected," She said. Aubray had a point.

He probably had bigger injuries to deal with, but I figured I should stop by. I walked toward where Ryan had been doing first aid.

"Hey man," I said, grabbing his attention. Ryan looked up at me from where he had been organizing his first aid box. "Hurt myself. Wanna clean it up?"

"Yeah, totally man."

"You come across any major injuries?" I asked.

"No nothing so far. I'm guessing those with big injuries have gone to a hospital." He took some gauze, tissue, and rubbing alcohol out of his bag and then glanced at my leg again.

"You're gonna need to shave it before I do anything. There is too much hair."

"There isn't even that much," I said.

"The bandage won't stick." Ryan said.

"Have you really been shaving legs all day? Or are you messing with me?"

"No, I'm being serious. And honestly, most of the locals don't have hair." He handed me a disposable razor as he tried to hide the grin on his face. "I'll admit, it's a little funny."

"Hey everyone, come watch!" Aubray yelled. "Owen's going to shave his leg!" A small portion of Quest had gathered to watch, setting their wood down in the pile nearby.

I ran the blade up and down my leg, clearing a path for Ryan to put a bandage over the shin. When I was finished, he put a small band aid over it. I sat there for a moment, watching as kids lined up to get clothes out of the donation bins. Only a handful of kids were there, and no more were coming, despite being told by Sue to go tell their friends. Instead, each kid was hiding whatever they had beneath their t-shirts or by wearing four hats at once.

When instructed to tell more children, they would return with just one kid, and each of the group would ask for more, claiming they hadn't been there beforehand. It was funny to watch, but also sad, because they needed everything they could take.

Breakfast came soon. I was one of the first people in line for rations, despite the fact there were only five buns left in the bowl. I decided not to take one. Ryan stood behind me, noticing what I had done.

"Just take one," he said.

"No man. There isn't enough," I said.

"Just take one." Ryan said.

"You're just trying to make up for shaving my leg, aren't you?"

"So, you're gonna starve?" Ryan asked.

"I won't starve. I'll still have a bit of pasta," I said.

"How 'bout we split one?" He suggested.

"Okay," I said.

He picked up a bun and tore it in half, placing one half on his plate and the other half on mine.

After breakfast, the two women from Chile left to be evacuated by their government. They said their goodbyes. Stevenson and Flore were gone as well, without saying goodbye.

After breakfast, Don said to all of us, "We're going to check out the community around Haiti Arise. We'll be going to the goat farm as well."

Marc led the way as we left the compound. The first field we walked through had a cow, a couple of goats, and some people sitting under the shade of a large tree. A few mango trees stood, but there were no mangoes on or underneath them. Flies buzzed around the cow's head and body. Its ribs were showing, almost like you would expect from a stray dog.

On seeing Marc, one of the women who had been sitting in the shade of the tree got up and ran toward us. I didn't know what she was saying, but I could see she was distressed given her arm movements and tone of voice. He told us what she was saying as they spoke.

"She is saying there are no longer mangoes to eat. All of them have been collected after the earthquake. Some people here survive solely off of mangoes during mango season." They spoke for another sentence or two, but this time with no translations. Marc then carried on, with the rest of us at his heels.

Marc seemed to be well known in the community as someone who helped others, or at least, someone who was capable of helping others. As we walked, many people would rush toward him and tell him their story, asking for help all the while.

It was both an energizing and disheartening walk through the community. Everything we saw was new to us, which brought some smiles, but at the same time, everything was in ruins.

We continued along a beaten path until it crossed with another path. At the middle of the crossroads was a giant tree that put even the tallest of our group to shame. It's top spread out, covering the four paths in shade. We took the left path and continued on.

We came across a man standing on the wreckage of his house. A part of the wall toward the back remained standing, the roof clinging on to it as the other side touched the ground. All the other walls had collapsed, leaving the rubble he stood on sprawled about. Beneath the tin roof lay his belongings. There was a dresser, a table, a chest, a chair —most were intact, but some were broken. Even his bike was broken, its wheels twisted. He stared at us as we walked by.

Almost all of the houses were one story tall; a factor I realized later mattered greatly. A lot of them were unfit to live in and beyond repair. On the other hand, two houses we passed remained nearly untouched. Both were made of wood.

"The reason we have so many concrete houses is because we have many hurricanes. The concrete withstands the hurricanes. The wood does not last the hurricane season, but I see the wood has survived the earthquake, and the concrete has not. Nobody expected an earthquake," He said.

A large church had lost its front wall, creating a hill of debris in front of the structure. At the sight of the church, Jim stopped and spoke out loud in prayer. Perhaps the pastor had been imagining what it would be like to lose his own church.

As we kept walking, a group of children ran up, stampeding alongside us, most wearing huge smiles. I felt a hand grab at my mine. It was a little girl. I took it and looked around to see many of the children were grabbing at hands three times their size. Children's laughter filled the air, and we laughed along with them. A group of them surrounded Nicole. She bent down and lifted a kid up onto her back. It was cute how much they liked Nicole.

Most of them were surprisingly joyful, even after all that had happened, but some of them, usually the older ones, were more aware. In their awareness, they struggled to smile, not seeing the world in the same light as their joyful siblings.

Bryden took a photo of a group of kids and showed it to them. They were ecstatic. More of them huddled into a group, wanting another picture taken. It was like they had never had their picture taken before. Perhaps they hadn't.

Most of the kids stayed with us on the path to the goat farm. On our way to the farm, Marc told us stories of Haitians as he pointed to their houses.

"This man has eight children," he pointed to a man who was facing away from us, numbly leaning his head back in a wheelchair. "He can not take care of them."

"This woman," he pointed to a house that had lost its front door, only a padlock hanging off of a wooden pole, remained in its place. "She has a granddaughter who badly needs glasses, but cannot afford them." Story after story showed the struggle of locals in Grand Goave.

Toward the end of the village, we walked uphill. At the top of the hill, we were given a clear view of the goat farm. We had come to Haiti to work on a surrounding wall for the goat farm, but when we showed up, it was clear there was no hope for that.

The wall had been started before the earthquake, but any signs of progress had turned to rubble. Only sections of it remained standing. The mother goat hadn't run away because she was tied to a stump on the ground, and her kids stuck around. A cow was tied up in the goat farm, scrawny like the other one. I felt useless and hopeless seeing the wall destroyed. Everything was gone.

We had come to Haiti to fund the drilling of a well, and the money had been stolen. We had come to build the wall of a goat farm, but it had been brought down. All of the things we had to offer had been taken by the earthquake. We had come to help the Haitians, but instead we required their help. We were a burden. I was a burden. Our entire trip was a waste.

A ruined house on the side of the road.

A family and their cat near the goat farm.

The inside of a house on the way to the Grand Goave.

Children by the goat farm.

Two children by the goat farm.

A girl sucking her thumb.

8. A Need for Rice

We headed back to the compound on a different path from where we came. Some of the kids followed, while others ran the other way. As we walked back, some Haitian boys, who appeared our age joined us. They pointed at the cameras and made some flicking motions with their fingers.

"You want your photo taken?" Jodie asked, holding up her camera.

"Yes," one boy said. "With you." He placed his arm over Aubray.

Jodie took the photo. Pretty shortly, the Haitian guys were laughing.

"Photo with me," another boy said, putting his arm over Katie. Aubray, Katie, Jodie and Brooklyn laughed.

After the picture was taken, Jodie showed the boys the photo, their laughter built up, carrying on to the girls, as they pointed at the camera, speaking in Creole amongst themselves.

"Another photo," one of them said putting his arm around Aubray.

"Be my wife," one of them said.

"Marry me," another one said.

The girls laughed along as they continued to take pictures with the guys. After a good few photos and laughs we moved along, back to the compound. Some of them came with us.

"Hi, I am Little Johny," one of the boys said as we walked. Little Johny was skinny, but he was taller than me.

"I am Jean, and this is Olisha." Jean had a narrow face, while Olisha was tall with broad shoulders. The rest of us introduced ourselves to them.

"We are staying here at Haiti Arise," Little Johny said. "We are students here." They walked toward a tent that had been set up with a sheet and sticks.

"I wish we could do more than just hand out clothes and move rubble and wood," Nicole said.

"Why don't we put our money together and buy food for the locals? The money we brought for New York." One of my classmates suggested, immediately they were met with agreement.

All of us contributed. We ended up gathering $2500. I felt we could have raised more. While I had given all my money, I felt like others were holding back on how much they were giving.

What else can they spend it on? We're not going to New York anymore.

I felt a rush of anger and irritation. My jaw locked. I wanted to yell at my group for not giving all that they could. I wanted to hate them. But I knew fighting would make everything worse, and for that reason I held my tongue.

A truck entered Haiti Arise. Out of it stepped a man with a red hat and matching red backpack. Marc handed him the money we had pooled together. The transaction was quick, and he left.

About an hour later he returned, this time without the truck. He led the group of us to the road outside of the compound. With him were two trucks piled high with bags of rice and three other men.

The main man spoke with Marc, who translated.

"He says that the price of rice has inflated since the earthquake. Normally we could have gotten much more, but they could only afford 3600 pounds."

I looked at the back of the truck, which held fifteen-ten kilo bags of rice. It looked like a lot. Both trucks had *POLICE* written on them, followed by *Grd. Goave.* In the back of the truck, one of the police wore long, baggy shorts and a shirt, a chain, and a fedora. He held a small dagger that he used to cut open the bags of rice. In fact, none of the cops wore uniforms.

Marc spoke in English to the locals who had volunteered to help. "Spread the word that Haiti Arise is giving away rice. Tell people to bring whatever they can to collect."

I wondered why Marc spoke in English, but figured they were some of his students. We began to haul the rice from the truck on to the ground. By the time we had a few bags opened, twenty people had shown up.

At first, they were dispersed, surrounding the rice bags, each holding out their pots and pans. Marc yelled something pointing away from the bag. There was a lot of yelling. Two of the officers grabbed some of the locals, pulling them away from the bags of rice. Some of them contested, but only verbally. Marc yelled again. They began to stand single file. Squished, they stood, chest to back, back to chest. Nobody could afford to leave a little bit of room because it could mean they weren't going to eat.

Each moment, another person came running from down the road or a nearby house. Entire families showed up in desperate need of the food.

Aided by the cops and some of the students at Haiti Arise, each of us took turns handing out rice. I dipped a cup into the bag, pouring it into a woman's cupped t-shirt.

I had expected mostly cups, bowls, and pots, but they were carrying anything that could hold rice —hats, shirts, pants pockets, pans, plastic bags, even their own hands.

Each moment, another group of people came running down the road, giving it their all, leaping, swinging pots by their sides. Even once in a single file, a few people yelled and pushed each other and whenever it was their turn to collect rice they would argue, asking for more. Begging. Pleading. Desperate.

The students of Haiti Arise decided how much each person got. They were the communication. Generally, it was the same amount for each person, but the odd time they would tell us to give more to someone who they knew had a big family. An older man, carrying a straw hat, kept returning to the rice bags, avoiding the line. The volunteers yelled at him, pointing toward a house that was a short walk away.

"That's his house," Marc said to us. "He keeps coming back because he is close."

The older man yelled at them, holding his straw hat out, next to the rice bags.

Marc and the students yelled again. He moved away, watching from afar.

A woman came up and started talking to the students with a calm demeanor. They yelled at her. She screamed back, desperation in her face and waving her arms. I couldn't tell what she was saying, but it was obvious she needed more rice. A lot of people needed more rice. It didn't matter how many times they got turned down, if they could just get one more cup.

Bryden, Katie and my mom stood on a small hill directly above the rice handouts. It was a very small hill, but due to the flat landscape, they could photograph almost everything from where they stood.

A tall man with dreads yelled something in Creole at them. His arms were long, and his gestures were harsh, rigid movements aimed at those with cameras.

"Keep taking photos," Marc told them.

"I don't think we should," my mom said. "He doesn't want us to!"

"Keep taking pictures!" Marc said. "It is fine."

My mom and Bryden, after some hesitation, continued to take photos, but didn't dare to point it his way. The tall man yelled again as he lunged toward them. Two of the police officers jumped in his way, shoving him backward.

The tall man was strong, not budging. Instead, he relaxed his posture stopped yelling and walked away. Suddenly, he turned, yelling again and raising his fist to us. The police pushed him back. Marc and the main officer joined in on the yelling. I couldn't make out any of it, but tensions were rising, that much was obvious.

My mom and Bryden lowered their cameras.

"It is fine," Marc said. "Do not worry about him. Keep taking pictures. People need to see what is going on here."

The tall man yelled again. One of the officers pushed him. The tall man backed away, no longer yelling. Instead, he was pretending to have calmed down as he inched his way toward the hill. When he got close enough, the cop shoved him again.

The tall man yelled, shook his head, and turned to walk away. The officers talked amongst themselves.

Reluctantly, they continued taking photos. Every time he got too close, two officers would grab him and push him away, yelling something in the process.

The man was persistent in trying to pretend everything was fine as he tried to get closer to them. A police officer shoved him and yelled something at him. At that, the tall man started up again, pointing up at the cameras, yelling and pushing back at the officers. The man yelled one final thing, shook his head and walked away.

As I looked at the end of the road, I could see people, usually children, who had been sent by their families. They were running as hard as they could, sweat dripping down their faces, full of exhaustion, but knowing they had to keep going. Their lives may have depended on it.

The line continued to grow larger. Every couple of minutes I looked at the end of the road, only to see another couple people rounding the corner, running to get in line for rice. We finished another bag.

Eventually, it was clear there wasn't enough rice to continue to give it away at the rate we were going. There were too many people who needed to eat. Marc said something to the police. They began to restock the truck. As the officers loaded it, the locals started to yell, scream and cry out in desperation and starvation. Don yelled over them.

"We're going to continue giving rice. Anyone who doesn't feel like coming can head back to the compound. The rest of you get in the back of the truck."

A few of us got into the back of the pickup, while Don and Jim sat in the cab with a Haiti Arise student and two of the officers.

We pulled away, picking up speed and kicking up dust. A group of kids ran after us. They ran hard. As the truck kept driving the kids slowly fell behind, slowing their pace as the truck increased its own. Only one kid kept his pace, a boy wearing a Spiderman shirt.

One of the officers grabbed a stick from the floor of the pickup and poked the kid in the cheek with it. Both men howled with laughter. The kid ignored the stick, continuing to stare straight ahead as he ran beside the truck.

Tell them to stop.

I wasn't brave enough to follow through.

Mixing with their laughter, I began to laugh. Not because of what they were doing, but because I was in awe at his ability to keep going. I watched as the kid with the Spiderman shirt slowly fell behind the truck as it picked up more and more speed. But the Spiderman kid never slowed down, knowing he needed that rice to survive.

The road was full of loose gravel and pieces of walls and houses. Whenever we hit a bump, I flew up in the air, my legs and body rising with the truck. There wasn't enough strength in my legs or abs to keep me planted. Instead, I relied on my hands, which clenched as hard as I could. If we were going faster, I could have easily flown off.

After holding on to the best of my ability, we pulled off the road and parked at what looked like a camp, filled with improvised tents. Each made of blankets and tarps, supported by sticks found on the ground. We unloaded the back of the truck and again, distributed rice on an individual basis. Anxious, I looked behind us to see if the kid with the Spiderman shirt would show up. He did eventually. The line at the camp wasn't as big, but it continued to grow as more and more people streamed in from the road, learning of our new location.

An older woman from the camp walked up to us. Most of her teeth had fallen out, the remainder either yellow or brown, her back hunched, her hair matted and wiry, and her feet covered in a permanent layer of dirt. Her toenails were long and unclipped, and she had a wart on each of her big toes. A lot of the old people in Haiti that I saw had a similar fate. Their state of health and body were crumbling like the walls. We gave her some rice.

It quickly became obvious that we had the same fate as before, not having enough rice, not at the rate we were going. Marc spoke with Don.

"I am going to go. I have told the police to give the rice to specific orphanages and schools, the cooks will distribute it through the meals they already provide. If you or anyone wants to go with them, you can."

"I will," Don said.

"And I'll go from here to find internet," Jim said.

"Take Emmanuel with you." Marc said, as he turned to his student and said something in Creole. The young man stepped forward. "I will see you back at the compound."

The rest of the group got a ride back with Marc and an officer to the compound.

At first, I hoisted myself into the back of the pickup truck, struggling to get my leg on to the bed of the vehicle. I sat down, clenching on to the side, but readily reconsidered. I was tempted to say nothing, ashamed of asking for special treatment, but I didn't want to fall out of the truck. I forced it out.

"Would you guys mind if I sat up front with Don?" I asked. "It's just that the roads are bumpy, and last time I felt like I might fall out." My voice displayed a slight tinge of guilt.

"Bro," Skye said. "Nobody cares if you don't sit back here. Go sit with Don."

"Owen," Nicole said. "No need to explain yourself. None of us would mind."

"Thanks," I said.

Nicole pointed at me and then pointed at the cab of the truck. The cop said something and then motioned with his hand. It was fine. I joined Don in the back. We drove through the main village. It was the first time we had driven through the downtown part of Grand Goave.

More destruction. Stores and houses had lost their roofs and walls. Two story buildings had been turned into half a story. Not many were doing anything other than sitting around. Amongst the rubble at the edge of their homes, small camps of people sat with a large cooking pot over a stove. All of them watched as we drove by.

There was one group of a dozen or so people sitting around a fire. The cop car stopped and the police in the back filled up an empty pot that one of them had to offer. The group was all smiles after that.

As the drive continued, I thought about what it was going to be like back home. What was school going to be like? I thought of Don no longer being our teacher.

"What's it gonna be like, Don?" I asked, briefly turning from the devastation to look at him. "Teaching another class?"

He sat silent for a moment. "One of the things about being a teacher is allowing your students to grow so they can become independent. It's just a part of the job. As a teacher, you have to adjust to different students. Every year is different than the previous, but," he paused, "I won't ever forget this group. You'll always have a place in my heart. What we have been through together is something unforgettable."

Suddenly, we jumped in our seats, turning off the road, jumping in our seats at the change. I was glad I wasn't in the back.

At our next location, we set out to unload the bags of rice from the back of the truck. The owner of the orphanage approached us and asked what was going on. She spoke in English.

"We're here to give you this rice," said Don. "Where abouts are your cooks?" A smile lit up her face.

"Right over here," she said, leading the way.

The first thing I noticed was that the children were sitting outside, and it wasn't because of recess or snack time. It was because the buildings that surrounded them were filled with rubble. Most of them sat silently and solemnly as we passed, although a few of the children offered to help carry rice bags from the truck.

When we were finished the owner thanked us. We returned to the truck and again I got in the cab with Don. We drove for a few more minutes, witnessing the turmoil that the disaster had brought, before leaving the main road to what remained of a school. We dropped off a few bags of rice before returning to the truck again.

The police took us back to the compound, keeping a couple bags for themselves, and drove away, leaving us with two bags for Haiti Arise.

Jodie and Skye brought the bags over to Lucianna, who took them as a personal compliment. She beamed at the sight of the rice. She had already begun to prepare pasta by the time we returned, the rice simply served as a guarantee for the future.

Jonathan approached Skye and I, clearly eager to tell us something. He was shaking his head like he did when he was cringing about something.

"Earlier, I was walking when I heard some thirteen or something year old Haitian girl yell, 'Jon *regardez!*'" The girl was asking him to "look" where she was. "So, I looked over and she was buck naked, showering. Fuck off!" Jonathan kept shaking his head.

Skye and I burst into laughter.

"So funny, dude!" Skye said.

"It was so fuckin' stupid. I don't wanna see a naked kid."

"Bullshit, you liked it," said Skye.

"Yeah, she probably didn't even tell you to look," I joked.

"Yeah right," he said. "Not something I wanna see on my birthday."

"But every other day you'd be okay with that?" Skye asked, jokingly. Jonathan began to playfully throw his fists into Skye's belly. Skye tried his best to block them, curling over, laughing as he did.

"Wait, wait, wait." Jonathan stopped as Skye spoke. "You said she was showering? Where?"

"Yeah. Right over there."

At the sight of it, Skye and I smiled. The shower was right by the forest. Its walls were made of four feet tall sheets of plywood that were held up by two barrels of water.

Inside the shower was, a tin bucket, and a bar of soap. The ground below me was already a little muddy from water. I filled the bucket up about a third of the way and then poured it on myself, promptly using my hands to make sure my entire body was wet. Then I soaped and finished off by filling up the bucket a little to rinse off. It was brief, but enjoyable.

That evening, we had pasta for dinner. There were buns offered too, but I decided not to take one. As I was eating, Margaux came up to me.

"You want the rest of my bun?" She asked.

"No, I'm good," I said. My stomach disagreed.

"Here, Owen. Take it." Margaux said, holding it out. "I'm not even that hungry." I knew she was lying out of kindness.

"You sure?" I asked.

"Yeah. It's fine."

"Thanks," I replied. "You didn't need to."

"No problem." She smiled, sitting down next to me.

From where I sat, I could see most people's plates of food. Sage had taken a big plate of food. I could tell Cam had also noticed her big plate of food as his eyes kept darting toward her. His lips were pressed together, and his face firm. Or perhaps it was because he hadn't smoked in many days. He looked at her again.

"Sage, why'd you take so much food?" He asked, bluntly.

Sage defended herself. "What're you talking about?"

"You're the smallest person here and yet you have the biggest fucking plate," Cam said.

"Chill out man," Sage said.

"I'm not gonna chill out when there are Haitians starving," Cam said. "The more you take, the more they don't have. You've seen what it's like out there."

"It's not that much." Sage said. "Chill out."

"Shut the fuck up okay?" Cam said. "Seriously, you're telling me to chill out when there are starving people everywhere. People would kill for that plate. That shit matters."

"Wow! What's up your ass Cam? Chill out, seriously man."

Cam stared at her for another moment, abruptly stood up and walked away. Jon and Skye followed him.

"Wow! What was that all about?" Sage said, looking around for a reaction out of any of us. "If he wanted some, he could've asked me."

I could feel my temper slipping as well. Cam and Sage were hungry. We all were. But if we had been starving, like many Haitians who knows how things could have gone.

Outside of Haiti Arise, handing out rice.

Marc, in the center of the photo, raising his arm to the tall man.

A line up of locals waiting for rice.

Locals waiting patiently for rice.

9. The Sound of Rescue

It had been four days, and with each day, people became more and more irritable. It wasn't just me and my group. Marc told us there had been a lot of looting outside of the compound as well as the ten grand stolen from the safe.

A few loyal Haiti Arise individuals, including Little Johny, volunteered to patrol the premises during the night. Other than the small patrol group and people's morals, there was nothing holding people back. The wall had fallen.

A side of the wall had fallen, so a bunch of the guys used planks of wood to lever it up, pushing, positioning it so it was even with the rest of the wall. They left the planks of wood there, acting as a support to keep it from falling again. Pink hibiscus flowers flourished along the broken wall in a contradicting sort of way.

All of us lay in bed as Jim stood.

"Everyone listen up, I got access to the internet."

"That's amazing." my mom said.

"Good job Jim!" Nicole said.

"I've got two pieces of news. First things first, a group of a thousand people on Facebook has been made in support of our safe arrival back home," Jim informed us.

A reaction of awe came across the group. One thousand people was a lot, even if it was just online.

"Second," He said with a beaming grin, "the Canadian government will be coming for us tomorrow with helicopters. They know where we are, and they're coming to get us!" The group cheered at the news. We were going to be rescued!

As Skye and I laid in bed attempting to find rest, our mom whispered from a few beds down.

"Hey Skye and Owen." She waited for us to look at her. "Think of Taya. Imagine what she must be thinking right now."

Shit.

I had yet to think of my sister or anyone at home, my only thought of back home had been when I talked to Don while delivering rice. I had been caught up in Haiti and the earthquake. As I lay, I thought about my sister and my dad and my friends.

Again, at four, the crickets fell silent and the earth began to shake. Most of us ran from the shelter, except for Katie and Brooklyn who were hiding under the church benches. The newborn baby cried.

Running from our beds at 4:00a.m. had become a routine, customary to our bodies, a tradition to have our hearts racing, scared our lives.

The next day, in the afternoon, someone yelled.

"They're here! I can hear them!"

The group erupted in cheers and yelling over top of each other. "We're being rescued!"

It took me a few moments longer, but I heard them as well. I heard the beat of helicopters.

There was a rush of excitement and yelling amongst some of the Quest group. The excitement increased as the helicopters grew nearer. We're going home! I felt a great sense of relief. A smile grew on my face. I looked over at the Haitians, who sat solemnly, clearly not undergoing the same fate. When the helicopters came into view, some of my group started to jump and wave at the choppers and Sage danced around in excitement. I was happy for us, but I didn't jump around or act excited. Not because I didn't want to leave, but because when I looked over at the rest of the people staying at Haiti Arise, the people who weren't leaving, I felt like shit. Unlike us, they weren't going anywhere. Unlike us, nothing was changing. There was no rescue from the very country they lived in.

I guess I had an advantage, though. Some of the people in my group were celebrating because they were finally going to see their family after all this time, where I had my twin and mom in Haiti with me.

The chopper was in our vision for a while, but it made no attempt to land. They flew right passed Haiti Arise.

"Where the fuck are they going?" someone yelled.

Maybe they were just turning around or looking for a place to land? But there was room to land at Haiti Arise. All of us stood, watching the sky in the direction they had gone. The sound of the helicopters became faint, eventually leaving us with nothing but the memories of the sound of rescue.

I was hit with despair as I realized we weren't being rescued. Some of the group was swearing in anger, or just sitting down in sheer disappointment.

We waited around, unsure of what to do. Surely, another helicopter would come. Someone yelled. Others joined in.

"They're here! They're here!" Shortly, I heard the beating blades of helicopters approaching. The smiles that had disappeared were back.

Above us, were two helicopters, flying nearly side by side. Again, I was rushed with excitement and relief. Again, people were jumping and waving their arms as the choppers drew closer in an attempt to grab the pilot's attention. And again, the Haitians sat solemnly on the benches, knowing they had nothing to celebrate about.

Despite our distinct location, the helicopters flew past Haiti Arise until the image of them was no longer in our view. As they continued to fly farther and farther away, the beating of the chopper blades became fainter and fainter, before diminishing completely.

They aren't coming for us.

We just had to be patient. Eventually, one would come for us. From then on, we were much more unfriendly toward what sounded like rescue, it no longer meant the inevitable safety that it had once promised. After all, we were not the only people who needed rescue. The helicopters continued throughout the day; sometimes they passed close to Haiti Arise, other times we couldn't see them, only hear their misleading taunts of escape.

Eventually, it became clear that, for some reason, we weren't being rescued. Still, we waited around, doing nothing but talking in the subtle hopes that the Canadian government would come for us. Later, we found out the helicopters that had passed us were rescue teams from other countries.

Ludcie, Lucianna's daughter, came up to a group of us. "My mother wants to show you something." Lucianna waved at us to follow her. A group of us followed her over to the main building where a shed-like building stood at its side. It was padlocked shut. In Lucianna's hand was a key. As she opened the rough shed doors, a quiet passed over the group of us. It was evident that before the earthquake hit, the shed had acted as a shop for artwork and supplies. Most of the plates and artwork had shattered. Shards of broken glass and ruined artwork was all over the floor. Some of the shelves that had been attached to the wall by L-brackets had tumbled over, sending all of the goods on top of them to the ground. Anything that could break had broken.

Lucianna stood still, staring ahead. After a moment, she gestured for us to enter. She knelt down and began picking up the shards of glass, placing them in her palm before tossing them in a nearby bin. A few followed, picking up glass and throwing it in a bin.

It was a small place, meaning we went in groups of three of four at a time. She sold all sorts of things: beaded necklaces, colored green, yellow, red and blue, Haitian booklets, multi-colored plates and bowls, and long machetes. There were even two milk crates full of old-school glass bottles of coke.

The cook became livelier as more of us handed her money, in exchange for what she had to offer. A few people bought machetes and necklaces, and most got a bottle of coca cola. After visiting the broken shop, my mom, Skye and I sat in a circle. I was picking at the grass in the field, twirling each strand between my fingers. I was irritated as I looked at Skye, who wore a new necklace.

"So, the rice yesterday, why didn't you guys give all your money toward it?" I asked, still annoyed by the fact that we could have given more rice. It didn't help that we weren't being rescued, either.

"Wait dude," Skye said. "You gave all your money?"

"Yeah."

My mom replied enthusiastically, "That's really great of you! I'm so proud of you! But did it ever cross your mind that we might need some money to get home?" It hadn't. "We might need to buy food or pay for a ride to the airport."

Shit.

I hadn't thought everything through. I had been stuck on this idea that my group was being selfish, when in actuality, they wanted to assure their way home.

"Don't worry, though," my mom continued. "We can share what money I have left for the ride back."

"Yeah same dude," Skye added. "I'll totally help out."

"Thanks, guys." My mom moved closer, peering at my chin. "Owen, I think I see some red at the end of your beard."

"Wait, what?" I asked.

"Come closer." After a brief inspection my mom continued, "Yeah, those are definitely orange tips at the end of your beard."

"What the hell!" I said. "I don't want a red beard."

"Ha," Skye forced out a laugh. "Dude! That's so funny. You've got a red beard! You're a ginger!"

I shook my head in amazement, knowing he hadn't thought before he spoke.

"Skye," my mom said. "You're twins." The three of us laughed.

Nicole, Margaux and Ryan played soccer with some of the local kids maneuvering around the ball with ease. The children ran around excitedly, showcasing some of their own footwork. Jonathan and Skye played cards with Jean Claude, Little Johny and Olisha. Instead of socializing, I sat and wrote. I wanted to get all of what had happened down on paper.

I stopped writing as the light began to fade. With journaling no longer an option, I headed over to a group.

"Why do they call you Little Johny?" I asked.

"I wish they did not." He laughed, not answering the question.

We were interrupted by the roar of motorcycle engines. I stood up, to see headlights piercing through the dark, bringing light to the field. Everyone was standing watching to see who was there. From where I stood, I couldn't see much. We walked closer, toward the light that shone from the bikes. Don and Marc went to talk with them. A few minutes later, the people on motorbikes drove away, leaving Don and Marc to tell us what was going on.

"Who were they?" Jodie asked.

"Workers from the U.N," Don said. "They had come to ask us if we knew anything about help and aid."

The United Nations, one of the biggest organizations in the world, had come to ask Marc if he knew anything about aid. It showed how little communication and info there was out in Haiti's countryside.

"What else did they say?"

Don paused for a moment, perhaps thinking of how to tell us the news.

"They said there's a chance of an earthquake larger than the first one hitting tonight."

10. The Devastation of Port au Prince

A chill crawled down my spine. *Fuck, we may not make it.*

None of us wanted to hear about the possibility of another earthquake, especially one larger than the first. A lot of people started talking over each other in a sort of panic.

"What are we gonna do?" someone asked amongst all the talking.

"We'll move out from inside the church," Don said. We dragged what we had from underneath the wooden church and into the fields of Haiti Arise.

The mother and her children remained inside the church, perhaps believing in its proven ability to remain standing.

As we lay down, Sage said, "I love you guys."

"Love you guys."

"Love you."

Everyone was saying it.

"I love you guys," I said.

I shut my eyes and prepared for the worst. I was confident we were going to be rescued the following day, but unsure of how our last night in Haiti might end.

The crickets fell silent and the earth began to ripple. I lurched out of sleep, ready to run. Instead, I crouched covering my head out of instinct, afraid it would lead to the predicted earthquake.

The field was full of yelling in Creole. When it stopped, there was a relative silence. We waited to see if there was more. Our last night in Haiti, and once again we were scared for our lives.

Had that been the earthquake? Or was it still going to come?

"What time is it?"

"It's four in the morning." Rachel said. I lay in bed my heart pounding, thinking of what could be, before sleep crept up on me.

The next morning, we didn't eat, under the impression we were being rescued sometime soon. Any food we could have eaten would have taken from those who were staying in Haiti.

Marc and some people had dragged benches out from the wooden church, placing them in neat rows in the field. They also brought out a microphone and speakers, placing them in front of the rows of benches. And finally, from inside the church, they dragged out a drum set, which I had failed to notice before.

It was then that I realized what they were doing. They were going to have a church service.

Some of the local girls were braiding each other's hair into thin rows in preparation for church. Aubray, Brooklyn, Katie, and Jodie greeted them, asking if they could get their hair braided as well. The local girls were enthusiastic and went on to braid each of their hair, weaving it from one side to another.

Skye went up as well, a big grin on his face.

"Can I get my hair done as well?" he said, pointing to his hair. The Haitian girls laughed.

"You want this?" asked one of them.

"Yeah," Skye said.

111

"Okay. Sit," she said. "I will give you when I am done with her." She grabbed strands of hair and weaved them around each other.

More and more people were entering the field, sitting down on the benches laid out for them. Groups of people were hugging and talking, waiting for the service to begin.

"A helicopter! They're here!" Sage yelled.

Shortly, I heard it too. Within no time, it was in my view, hovering over Haiti Arise. Others from my group were jumping and yelling, excitedly trying to grab its attention. We were finally going to be rescued! It descended, causing bursts of wind to come from all around, landing in an open area of Haiti Arise.

Two men dressed fully in orange search and rescue gear and covered in straps, wearing big backpacks came out of the helicopter.

"We're here to pick up the most injured!" one of them yelled over the beating of the chopper.

Sue's ribs still hurt and she was older. Over the beating of blades, it was hard to hear what they were hollering at her.

"When are the others coming?" my mom asked. "They'll be here soon," the younger looking one responded. They put a special suit on Sue, and then walked her toward the helicopter, Sue's hair flailing wildly the closer she got. Then the helicopter took off, leaving a massive gust of air and most of us with a sense of confusion. Obviously, they knew where we were, but where were the rest of the rescue choppers? Locals were still arriving for the religious service, climbing and stepping over the broken wall. The benches were packed when Marc started up the generator.

I was surprised he had turned on the generator just to use the microphone, but I suppose for him and the people there, church was a priority.

Marc spoke into the microphone. I hadn't known Marc was a pastor until then. Hands raised and voices cheered to whatever it was he preached in Creole. Sometimes people yelled back, an "Amen", "Hallelujah," or something in Creole.

Then the singing started, filling the air with a hearty gospel. All of the locals readily joined in on the singing. Even some of the children joined in. Amidst the singing, two vans rushed into Haiti Arise, kicking up a storm of dust as they came to a halt.

Nine soldiers stepped out of the two vans, followed by a few reporters. Each militia held a large rifle with one arm, broadcasting their strength. All of them wore helmets, safety glasses or sunglasses, and thick camouflaged military gear. Behind them, the media held microphones, shouldered massive cameras and dispersed quickly to start covering their story.

It brought a strange contrast. On one side, the military and the media, on the other side, a church full of singing poor people. One side was clean, the other dirty, one wore gear, the other donated clothes, one side held guns and cameras, the other side held children.

A soldier stepped forward. I could only assume he was the leader of the military group.

"Alright everyone, get your stuff. Say your goodbyes. And let's get on out of here. Alright, now where's the teacher? I need to speak to the teacher," the corporal commanded more than he asked, his voice louder than the preacher.

Don walked up to him. The two shook hands. He had a striking resemblance to our teacher, with a thick mustache and a similar body shape.

"We don't have enough room for everyone in the two vans. There are a lot more Canadians here than we expected, so we're leaving it up to you to decide who stays and who goes."

"Will there be enough for the kids?" Don asked. We were his main concern.

"Yes. And more, there just won't be enough room for everyone here. Is anyone in your group badly injured or have any health issues we should know about?"

"Well, an older woman from our group was hurt, but she was air-lifted out earlier."

"Alright, there are a lot of people waiting to get home at the embassy. Your group could spend a long time waiting there. The airport is in shambles, there are no regular flights going. Only military. Again, it'll take time to get on a plane. As for the drive to the embassy, we'll have to take precautions. The roads are in bad condition. It's going to be a long drive, and a lot of homeless and injured people sit on the side of the road."

The corporal continued to inform Don of what laid ahead. "If we come under an attack of any kind, be ready to duck and take cover. I'll make sure my men inform the kids of the same once we load the vans. As for the dead bodies, we're lucky because they moved almost all of them yesterday."

"They've been moved?" Don asked.

"Yes, they're now stacked on street corners. Before, many of the bodies hadn't been touched, laying where they had died. We've mapped out a route to avoid most of it."

A silence fell across the group. He continued, "Now once we get to the embassy..."

I stopped listening, moving away toward one of the old donation bins, which had already started to fill with our old clothes. I took everything out of my bag, except the papers I had journaled in and my winter jacket, assuming it would be of no use in Haiti. I threw my clothes in the bin. That was my farewell. I didn't want to say goodbye to anyone. It wasn't that I was bad at goodbyes, but I didn't need to say it to anyone. I just wanted to hurry, get in the van, and leave Haiti.

The news reporters tried to get interviews or walked around getting pictures of Haiti Arise.

There was a general feeling of guilt and hopelessness for the locals we were leaving behind. A lot of tears flowed as people said farewell.

Ryan gave Richardson his clothes, as well as his email address and phone number so they could keep in touch. Some of the group spoke into the microphone, making promises to raise funds for them as soon as we got home. All of us made plans and promises to fundraise. Bryden, being an avid player of the drums, performed a solo, which got some of the locals cheering.

Skye hugged Little Johny. As they did, their hands stealthily swept one another's as Skye passed over a handful of money.

"*Mesi.*" Little Johny thanked him in Creole. "I will tell nobody."

Skye wiped his eyes turned, meeting my gaze with his own. As I watched Skye, I felt guilty for not showing as much empathy. He had certainly spent more time getting to know some of the locals than I had. I walked over to Little Johny and said goodbye, hugging him.

"You two will return soon?" Little Johny asked.

"Yeah," Skye said.

"Alright, let's start getting into the vehicles!" A soldier commanded. I reached the van. At the door, I was greeted by a trooper holding a clipboard.

"Name?" he asked.

"Owen Spears."

"Okay." He waved me through. "Go on."

I followed the orders taking a step up.

"Name?"

"Skye Spears," I heard behind me.

We sat down together toward the back of the van. Kyler also got into the same van as us. He was wearing a white suit with a matching cowboy hat. I didn't know where he got it from, but I didn't like it.

Marc got into the van as well. He planned on going to Canada to see his family, including the new addition. I couldn't say the same for the vacationers. Later, I found out that a chaperone from Haiti Arise offered to drive those left behind to the embassy. Nobody knows what happened to Patrick, Barbara and their kid.

Through the bus windows, reporters asked the group questions as other reporters came on to the van. One reporter stood at the front of the bus, grabbing most people's attention as he said a few words.

"Before the earthquake, Haiti had nothing and now they have less."

A different reporter greeted me.

"Mind if I ask you a few questions?"

"No. My name is Owen Spears," I replied, knowing she was going to ask for my name anyway.

"How did you feel when the earthquake hit?"

"Scared," I replied, honestly.

"Why did you feel scared?"

What a stupid fucking question.

I wanted to hate her. I felt like yelling at her, calling her stupid and a lot of other things, but I refrained from it, knowing the real reason I was angry had nothing to do with her. I was hungry, tired and stressed. After a moment of silence, she rephrased the question. Maybe she could tell I wasn't going to reply.

"What was going through your head when the earthquake hit?"

"Hopefully we don't die."

"Wow." She took a moment. "And what about your thoughts after the earthquake?"

"I don't know," I said. I didn't know how to describe the feeling. "I was just kind of in shock."

"Anything else you would like to say?"

I hesitated for a moment. Quoting the previous reporter, I said, "The Haitians had nothing before the earthquake, now they have less."

"Thank you."

Another reporter asked Katie a question through the window.

"What did you see?" Katie remained quiet for a moment and then burst into tears as she struggled to reply.

As the military wrapped up their preparations, they began to board the bus. Once all the interviews were wrapped, a military officer introduced himself.

"My name is Master Corporal Good Fellow." Skye and I laughed a little.

Skye raised his voice. "Is that really your name?"

The man stared at him sternly. "Yes." He carried on as if nothing had been said.

"If you hear gunfire, duck immediately and cover your head! If the bus is stopped, do not get out unless ordered! If we leave the bus, do not follow unless ordered! Does everybody understand?" He paused, not truly waiting for a response. "We'll be handing out masks and a cream to cover up the smell. We highly recommend that you wear the masks and place the tiger balm under your nose to hide the stench of bodies."

A soldier walked down the aisle, holding out a cream. I don't think any of us took the tiger balm.

A couple rows ahead, a man in full camo and a helmet sat down. He turned back toward us, smiling.

"How are you guys?"

"Why don't you have a gun?" Skye asked.

"I'm a minister. My job is to comfort you. If you want to talk about anything, I'm here for you."

As interviews came to a close and preparations wrapped up, the van started, driving through the opened red gate, leaving the locals with clouds of dust to remember us by.

From then on, I was quiet, wrapped in an imaginary heavy blanket, that weighed down on my entire body.

The road was empty. The highway had been cleared of rubble, except for a large boulder that amounted to the size of our van, taking up half the road. We slowed down as another vehicle drew near, letting them pass before we continued. By the side of the road, makeshift tents had been set up, using blankets or sheets, but still left people sleeping on the ground.

Thirty minutes into the drive, we passed the town of Leogane. "The epicenter of the quake wasn't far from here," one of the reporters said. "They're saying Leogane got hit the hardest. That, and Port au Prince."

People were moving, carrying water, or cooking rice or pasta with large pots over open fires. Laundry dried over strings that went between the remains of two buildings. I could only assume that before some of the clothing had been stained with blood from the unforgiving earthquake.

At another point, the entire highway was smooth, almost untouched, except for a small crack in the road. I peered down, the gap in the road led into the ground, as if the earth had been ripped in two.

Even though we practically had the highway to ourselves, the drive felt long. Each moment brought new images of what mother nature was capable of.

Hour Four

Eventually, we reached the Port au Prince dump which was the same as it had been beforehand —a wasteland with spots of burning garbage, a landmark that meant we were about to enter the capital city. At this point, the van slowed.

Jeannette Rankin, a U.S. politician, once said, "You can no more win a war than you can win an earthquake."

I've never been in a war, but nobody could deny the latter part of what she said after seeing the devastation of Port au Prince. There was no winning an earthquake. And the poverty had allowed the disaster to flourish, a hibiscus flower of destruction.

If Haiti had been poor beforehand, then I didn't know what it had become now. It was, in many aspects, gone, a ruin of a place that we had seen only a week before.

I couldn't smell anything from the van, but a lot of people shielded their faces with a medical mask or folded bandana or toothpaste under their noses to cover up the stench of the bodies. The worst was seeing a kid with toothpaste under their nose, knowing they had smelled them -knowing they had seen them. Although the military had mapped out a way to avoid the dead, a few people in the group said they saw them. That they had been piled, limp bodies, stacked by the dozens in alleyways.

Outside a gas station, a massive crowd gathered, easily a hundred people with jerry cans in their hands waited to use the pump. The price of rice had skyrocketed in Haiti, I could only assume the same for gas and other necessities.

The road was no longer empty, and it wasn't just locals crossing desperate to do something. Some people stared at us as we drove by, but most people were trying to keep busy, getting gas, cooking rice, collecting water, drying laundry. In the backs of trucks, aid workers chucked out water bottles. Each aid truck bore a different flag. It seemed as though every country had come to help.

Doctors Without Borders and the Red Cross, set up huge temporary medical tents that had many people coming and going, waiting and staying. If there had been a hospital nearby, it was now diminished to rubble. A man carried crutches. A woman used another pair, hobbling as she walked.

Masses of tents were so extreme that there was an area called Tent City. Each tent held a family, or a person, and there were rows and rows of them, each matching in shape and despair. The city was in survival mode, public services shut down, a bus stop was repurposed into a tent by a blanket being hung over it. What had once been a park for kids to play in was now a camp of tarps for the homeless. The play equipment and surrounding fence draped with clothing that needed to dry.

Tents were replacing everything. They were being set up anywhere and everywhere and were only going to increase as time went on.

Diggers and other construction vehicles drove around, attempting to move rubble. There was a lot of it, and not many diggers. The idea of ever clearing all the wreckage was impossible.

We, and the few other drivers, wove in and around the littered roads, making the drive last hours. Vehicles remained empty, stationary at awkward angles; their drivers having pulled over in hurried attempts to avoid facing the earthquake from inside. We drove by a van that was mangled, the rear of its roof collapsing in on itself, its doors twisted to the point of no return. Car windows had been smashed, either by looters or debris. Some cars were even flipped due to the sheer power of the earthquake.

In the countryside, few people had to be dug out from beneath buildings because most were only a story or two tall, but I could see that the city was much different. I was told later that structures collapsing on people had been the main cause of death. The

Haitians ran into their homes, thinking it would bring them safety, but their homes were poorly constructed, causing many to die.

People walked on the broken buildings, throwing rubble in a search for things to collect, or someone.

Some buildings looked like they had gone through a landslide, a mass of rubble, rebar and furniture pouring out in one direction. Electrical wires had become entangled or broken by the collapse of their poles. Concrete slabs of roof and wall blocked alleyways. Most houses remained standing, but many, I had to assume, were unstable to live in. Wires of rebar, torn apart during the quake, stuck out from many of the pieces of concrete.

One building, however tall it had been before the earthquake, had fallen, leaving a sea of debris and household items. What looked like a family of six, stood on one of the only parts of the havoc that remained intact -a small slab of cement. One of them was searching for anything of value that they could salvage amongst the wreck. The mother, sitting on a bucket with a pot in her hand, looked as though she had been crying for days. The family had collected some essentials to survive, cooking supplies mainly, which sat on the foundation with them. They were living on that platform, with the outline of their home surrounding them.

It wasn't just houses.

A school that read "Kindergarten" with lots of paintings of Disney-like characters looked beaten up from the inside. Sometimes I couldn't tell what a building had been because of the extent of damage. A man carried a case of coke from a pile of remains that might have been a convenience store.

We passed by some of the same buildings we had seen before the earthquake. The church with the children's choir was crushed, its roof collapsed. I could only hope the singing children had left before then.

The Haitian Parliament building still remained, but was far from functional. Most of its roof had fallen through. The dome at the top had fallen forward, piercing the structure. Many of the pillars that had supported it stood at an angle, ready to fall if it weren't for all the rubble surrounding them, supporting them. Remains of the building blocked the entrance. Massive chunks of the parliament building laid broken. Once a large majestic building, the earthquake had brought it to ruin. Many government workers had passed during the event, what Richardson had said was true. Haiti had no government.

There was no hope for Haiti. There was barely even a government to fix it. What we saw left us with a sense of hopelessness and guilt, but the scenes of destruction came to an end, as we arrived at the Canadian Embassy.

Don talking with the military.

A tent on the way to the capital.

Two men wearing masks in Port au Prince.

A group of tents in Port au Prince.

A destroyed building in Port au Prince.

A family standing on their destroyed home.

A massive building turned to rubble.

A car crushed by a nearby building.

11. The Embassy

We pulled up to the great fortress of an embassy. Its massive walls appeared untouched by the powerful earthquake and its many aftershocks. We waited outside for a moment as the two layers of giant metal gates opened, allowing us to pass through. All of us got out of the van to see Sue waiting, smiling. After a few of us hugged her, she spoke.

"The medics told me I have a few broken ribs."

"It's good to see you," Don said.

"It's horrible out there," the secretary said.

By the time we made it to the embassy, the day had turned into evening. The sun was still shining, but given that it was winter, it would fall soon.

"Hello everyone," a person said. "I work with the embassy. Please follow me to get registered." She brought us to a table covered in papers where two people sat.

It took a while for them to run through all of our names and Don did most of the talking. We waited in line to be called up. A couple of the guys and I got mad at Kyler for wearing a white suit. We all took our turns.

"Dude, why the fuck would you wear that shit?"

"I brought a suit down with me. I'm gonna wear it," Kyler said.

"You're such a piece of fucking shit. Is this a fucking joke to you? People are dying and you're prancing around in a fucking white suit and cowboy hat."

"Fuck you. I brought it. I'm gonna wear it," he said.

"You make us all look like fucking assholes!"

"Kyler, you're a douche. Take that shit off!"

"No man. I brought it down. I'm wearing it once," he replied, turning away.

Nearby, a few tents had been set up that were fenced off. A sign read *MEDIA*. A group of reporters walked toward us holding out microphones for anything newsworthy. A man holding just a pen and paper asked for my name, and then said,

"Are you glad it's over now?"

"It's not over."

It didn't feel over. It wasn't for me, and it certainly wasn't for those who lived in Haiti.

Once registered, we found a place to sit on the ground as a group. I sat down for a bit, amongst the light chatter of the group.

Fuck this.

I wanted to be alone. I didn't want to speak with anyone. I stood up and started walking around. The main embassy building was stable, I didn't see a single crack along the thing. It had long glass windows, which made it easy to see inside. Paperwork lay scatted about, chairs were flipped over and a number of computers lay on their side. It was abandoned, leaving everything as is, and given the state of it, I doubt anyone had made the trek back in.

The embassy had an array of tents; a first aid tent, a place where food was handed out cafeteria style and a tent where the military was staying. The soldiers played cards and smoked in the shade, trying to avoid the sun.

Hundreds of people were in the embassy, walking around or waiting in line for food. It was chaotic and busy. In hopes of getting food, I joined the line. Next to the food tables was a large pool, covered with a tarp. A few pieces of litter sat on the tarp. The closer I got to the end of the line, the smaller the portions became, quickly becoming mere spoonfuls. I studied the mash with eyes like a hawk. I wasn't sure if there would be enough for me.

The ladle was now scraping the bottom, barely managing to find any scraps. My stomach rumbled. I watched as the person ahead of me got the last of the dish. I held up my Styrofoam bowl in hopes that she would have hidden food stowed away.

"I'm sorry, that was the last of it," the woman said as she started to stack the dishes. "We'll be serving more shortly." Spontaneously, I gave up my spot, making my way back to my group. At the end of the line I saw Margaux and my mom.

"Hey guys."

"Hey. Did you get any food?" my mom asked.

"No. They just ran out. I was right behind a guy who got served."

"Do any of you want this?" A stranger said. He held out a bowl of stew. "I'm not hungry. I just ate."

I didn't believe him. Maybe he had just heard our conversation and was being a good guy, or maybe he genuinely had just eaten.

"Are you sure?" I asked him, still unsure myself.

"Positive. I'm not hungry."

"Oh, okay." It wasn't an opportunity I could refuse. I took it from him. "Thank you."

"You're welcome." He walked away.

There wasn't much, but it was more than any of the other portions we had in Haiti. I looked between Margaux and my mom.

"Which one of us should take it?"

"You should," Margaux said. "You were supposed to get food anyway."

She looked over at the wide open kitchen. "They just started serving again." I didn't know why I hadn't just stayed at the front of the line.

"Alright. Thanks." I shoveled down the stew while waiting with them. The chunks of beef tasted incredible, the salty mush engulfed my mouth.

My mom looked at the pool with desire. "Why isn't anyone swimming in that pool?" My mom asked jokingly, but with some sincerity. "It would be so nice right now!"

A man in front of us turned around.

"It used to be for swimming. That was before the earthquake. Now it's the only water they've got."

"Wow, really?" my mom asked.

"Yes. That's the only water at the Canadian Embassy right now, so they have to conserve it all for drinking. What I heard was a little over five hundred Canadians are registered with the embassy. It means that the embassy recognizes five hundred Canadians live in or are currently visiting Haiti, but the reality is that five thousand Canadians are in Haiti, ten times what they expected. The embassy has got to be conservative, knowing only more Canadians are going to come."

"Wow," my mom said. "That's bad."

"And," he said, "they don't know how long they'll need this water for. Could be ages."

My mom and him continued talking. "Owen," my mom said after a moment. "He's from the same town as my Papa. Him and my dad grew up together."

"Small world, eh?" the man said with a laugh.

"It really is," I said.

"And what're you doing here?" My mom asked.

"Well, every year I come down and provide bicycles for people. I run a little repair shop down here." The man ahead of us got his food. "Anyway," he said, "was nice meeting you."

"You too," my mom said.

We headed back to the Quest group, who had settled on a hill overlooking a number of outhouses. Everyone was sprawled about, sitting, or laying down, waiting for any news of going home. It was already getting dark.

Around midnight, a flashlight wavered from person to person and a voice said. "Come with me. We're ready," Sleepily we followed a man gathering around the tarp covered pool. A lot of people were already there, each person impatient to go home.

"If your name is called," the man at the other end of the pool said, "then you will take a bus to the airport and on to the next plane heading to Montreal." The people's names he called began walking toward the busses.

When we were registering our names to the embassy Don had spoken for a long time with the registrar. They told us we were going to be the number one priority, aside from the injured. But Don wanted more. We were his responsibility. All of us relied on him. He wanted all of us to go back home together.

And so, he made them promise that we were all going to be on the same flight.

A lot of names were called. Each time it was met with a sort of happiness. A freedom. They were finally going to be rescued. Finally, a name was called that I recognized. All of us cheered. It meant all of us were leaving.

Those that had bought machetes handed them over as we boarded the bus. I didn't think they were getting them back.

The bus ride to the airport was short. We were unloaded right onto the runway, immediately rushed with the overwhelming whir of planes. I had thought the helicopter rescue had been loud, but these dwarfed it in comparison. Each differed in size, yet all were massive at the same time.

Two lines of troops marched passed us, and went on for what seemed to be a hundred soldiers column, steady and at pace with each other. I expected to be lifted off the ground right away and flown home, however, that wasn't the case.

We sat on the concrete of the runway waiting for instructions. A soldier went from one person to the next, offering something that he held in his palm. When he got to me, I saw what they were. I grabbed a pair of ear plugs. They fit awkwardly in my ears, but they helped dampen the noises.

Some of the group spoke amongst themselves, but I didn't bother. I knew I wouldn't be heard, not over the deafening roar of the many military planes.

At last, a cluster of soldiers approached. I didn't hear what they said, but hundreds of us followed them, nearing a massive plane. I was in a sea of strangers, but kept going, following the soldier leading us. I was lost from my group, but paid it no attention, and just kept going with the huge crowd of survivors. As I walked toward the ramp up to the airplane, a man in an orange shirt patted me on the back while muttering a number as he kept count.

The ramp leading up to the plane made it look like we were entering the belly of a mechanical whale. The ceiling was at least as tall as a two story building.

Once aboard the cargo plane, soldiers instructed the hundred or more of us to sit on the floor in rows, squished against each other. I sat down with a thump. The seating was uncomfortable, but I didn't care, I just wanted to leave, to get out of Haiti.

Hour Four

On one side of me was an older man and on the other side a woman a few years older than me. Massive straps anchored to the deck stretched over ten of us per strap, like a giant seatbelt. Medical stretchers filled with the injured were stacked three and four high, placed like bunk beds in one of the corners. A few people tended to them.

It was crowded to such an extreme that it was hard to view anyone from my group, but I did manage to spot Jodie, Margaux and Marc. The young woman beside me and I started talking.

I asked her where she was from. It was hard to hear, but it must have been somewhere in Canada.

"Owen!"

Again. "Owen."

I looked a few rows over at Margaux who had been calling my name. She pointed toward a couple of troops looking around. Apparently, they had been asking for me. Elijah stood by their side, looking around as well.

I yelled, "Here," but the plane was too noisy to be heard. I raised my hand, like the student I was.

"Come with me," one of them instructed.

I was alarmed and confused, but knowing no better, I obeyed. The young soldier held out his hand to help me up. I took it. As he guided me toward the front of the plane, he switched his grip to my wrist.

I turned my head to see Elijah wasn't moving. In fact, he was taking a seat in my place.

What's happening? Why's Elijah staying? And why do they want me?

With each step, the soldier would offer words of encouragement. "Yeah, that's it" and "Watch your step."

I guessed to him I looked young. My arm felt light in his grasp.

"What's happening?" I yelled. He managed to hear me.

"I'm taking you to your mom," he said.

I was even more confused now. Why were we walking toward the front of the plane?

Near the cockpit, a small metal case of stairs led outside. The soldier took the steps down, then offered out his hand. I took it, but I didn't want to. Why are we leaving the plane? The atmosphere was deafened by the footsteps of marching troops and the roaring engines of military planes.

We kept walking, away from the plane, away from the marching soldiers. It was just the two of us now, on what seemed to be an empty air strip. We continued for another moment, stopping in front of an old, isolated city bus. He made a motion with his hand and the doors were opened.

"They're in there," he said. "Get in."

The soldier stayed on the pavement as the driver shut the doors behind me. I looked back to see them seal.

A few minutes later, the plane would take off. I was still in Haiti.

12. Montreal

I stood at the front of the bus, turning away from the recently sealed doors.

What the fuck is going on?

I turned my head to see eight people. Each of them had a blanket on top of their body. Curtis and Corrine cuddled toward the back of the bus. Aubray's head rested on Ryan's shoulder. Brooklyn and Katie looked up at me from their seats in a sleepy disgruntled acknowledgement, quickly closing their eyes again. Skye was there, and like the soldiers had promised, my mom.

I remained standing at the front, ready to leave, still unsure of why they weren't on the plane. My heart started racing. If we didn't get off the bus immediately, we were going to miss the plane.

The plane that will take us home.

"What's going on?" I asked, my voice composed despite my growing fear.

"I couldn't get on the plane, so I told the soldiers to go and get you," my mom replied, her voice calm as well. It was like when we were coming to Haiti, except instead of waiting to board for me, she was taking me off the plane. "I didn't want you to leave without me. We have to stick together as a family."

I was pissed. I just wanted Haiti to be over.

"Why couldn't you get on the plane?" I asked.

"'Cause there wasn't enough room." She sat up, continuing. "I pleaded with them to go grab you, but they refused, until finally Curtis," I looked over at Corrine and Curtis, the older couple who sat a few rows down, "Mentioned that you have a disability and then they agreed."

No wonder the soldier was treating me like a baby.

"So they traded Elijah for you."

I remained standing for a moment, looking around to see if everyone else had given up. I accepted my fate and sat down.

"How long until the next plane?" I knew I wasn't leaving anytime soon.

"I don't know," my mom continued, her tone fearful. "Hopefully before the next earthquake hits. Could be a couple hours, could be another day."

I was irritated. I wanted to be in a safe place, but quickly gave up all hope of leaving, settling down in one of the seats. I leaned my head back, shutting my eyes for a moment.

Without even realizing how the time had passed, I was awoken and told we were leaving by a camouflaged man standing at the front of the bus. The sun was just beginning to come up. I couldn't believe we had stayed another night in Haiti. The earthquake we had feared had not come.

The plane we boarded was much smaller than the one I had been on previously. Seats made of rope had been folded out from the side of the plane, resulting in a rigid hammock.

I thought of what I needed. I needed sleep, food and a shower. I wanted to sleep on the plane, but didn't know if I would be able to. My mom took out some pills from her bag, pouring them into her open palm.

"It's melatonin, a drug used to help you sleep," she said. The rest of the group took some. I hesitated.

"I don't really wanna take pills."

"It's completely natural," she informed me.

I took the thing from her, using my saliva to swallow it.

The rest of the flight was a blur.

When I opened my eyes, my mom handed me a cardboard box.

"It's food," my mom said. I was about to tear it open and start eating when she filled me in on the catch.

"Wait, don't open it," she said.

"What? Why not?" I asked.

"Because everything is boil in a bag. It's all military rations. You can't eat it unless it's cooked."

All of the excitement from my stomach disappeared. I was still mad at her for taking me off the plane; her telling me we had food then taking it back annoyed me even more. I drifted off again.

I opened my eyes to see a big ray of sunlight entering the plane where the ramp had been.

Are we home?

I stood up, groggily making my way toward the open ramp. It didn't make sense. Nobody else was moving. I looked down to see a runway with palm trees in the distance. A soldier ascended, boots clambering up the ramp, steadily holding an oval tray of hotdogs that had been cut into thirds. I hurried over.

"Can I have one?"

"Take a few," he said.

"Where are we?" I asked.

More survivors joined me at the head of the ramp, each grabbing at the hot dogs on the tray. But nobody grabbed more than a few, aware, of how little there were, and considerate of others. I snatched four of them, cradling them in my hands like a baby.

"We're on an island outside of Haiti," he said. "Just fueling up."

"What country is it?" I asked.

If he said its name, I didn't catch it. "It's actually owned by England," he said. "We'll be leaving shortly."

I returned to my group, offering those that were awake a piece of hotdog.

Almost as soon as I sat down, I fell asleep again, opening my eyes just long enough to notice the drool on my shirt before dozing off again.

I opened my eyes. This time I didn't feel as groggy. A lot of people were still resting. Skye lay on the open floor, his arms and legs sprawled out in every direction.

"Any news?" I asked those who were awake.

"They said we'd get there soon," my mom said.

I reflected on how our trip had been such a close call. First, our flight was pushed ahead, we ran through the airport, barely making it. We had only been in Haiti just over four hours when the earthquake hit. We had only been at Haiti Arise for forty five minutes before it all happened. And Haiti Arise is only a thirty minute drive from Leogane, the town closest to the epicenter.

Forty five minutes at Haiti Arise and thirty minutes from Leogane make up just over an hour. Meaning, if we had arrived to Haiti an hour later, if our flight hadn't been pushed ahead, we may have been driving passed the epicenter when the earthquake hit.

"We'll be landing soon," a soldier said, taking me out of my thoughts. "Please take a seat." Skye got off the floor, sitting down beside me. The plane dropped, and my stomach with it as we began our descent.

We landed, the plane vibrating on impact. The ramp unfolded, allowing sunlight into the aircraft. I looked out over the sea of heads to see snowflakes falling ever so slowly. I had almost forgotten about snow. We walked off, single file, receiving a Red Cross blanket from a soldier as my sandals crunched the lightly snow covered pavement.

They directed us to a city bus. The bus was about half full with all of the people who had been rescued, like us. A police car in front of us had its sirens blaring, lights flashing the red and blue. A cop car drove behind us as well. We were being escorted.

It was sunny out, but the Haitians rescued with us huddled up in their blankets, not used to the cold. Everyone was silent.

As we drove, I thought of the three things I needed again – food, sleep, and a shower. I had slept on the plane, so I could cross that off my list. The bus stopped at our destination, a high-end hotel in Montreal. I liked to think that Haiti was over because we had made it back, but I knew it wasn't.

I stepped out of the bus to see a lot of news reporters anticipating our arrival. They held out their microphones and shouted questions, but a blockade had been set up, meaning we entered the hotel free from the harassment.

The nine of us split from the other people on the bus as Don, Elijah, Jon and Kyler came up. They had all changed and showered and were clearly happy to see that we had made it. I was curious how long they had been waiting but didn't ask.

Close to tears, Don hugged me, planting a kiss on my forehead as he did so.

"I'm so sorry," Don said. "I had no clue. I didn't know you guys weren't on the plane until we had already taken off."

"It's fine, Don. It's not your fault," I assured him. A television was going off in the background. On it, the news anchor was talking about us.

"The seventeen youth have officially been reunited after being stuck in Haiti for six days. They slept on the ground for six days, with very little

food and water. Eleven of them arrived earlier this morning and the other six arrived just a few minutes ago. The high school group entered the country the day of the earthquake. They will be reunited with their family members tomorrow."

The majority of the media was in French because we were in Quebec, but some of the TVs and headings in the newspapers were in English. "High school group stuck in Haiti." Or "Grade twelve's in earthquake!" I caught some of the French, but not enough to understand.

"How'd you guys know we were here?" Ryan asked.

"The news is live," Jon said. "We saw you guys walking in."

"That's cool. How long have you guys been here?" Skye asked.

"A few hours," Kyler said, who had changed out of his cowboy suit.

Jon said, "Someone told the news that the six of you got left behind. When the media found out, they went berserk."

"That's crazy," I said.

"Yeah," Elijah said. "Crazy. They were flipping out." He laughed.

After talking for a little bit, Don guided us into a different room to a few people dressed in suits while we continued talking amongst ourselves.

Jonathan said, "There was an anchorman trying to bribe us to come outside 'cause the hotel won't let any of them in."

Kyler said, "The guy told me if I came outside, he would let me call my mom."

"And did you?" Ryan asked.

"Yeah," Kyler said. "But the hotel has phones we can use. I just felt like helping the reporter out. The man's got a job to do, you know."

Don and a man with a suit made their way toward us.

"This is Stockwell Day, the Minister of International Trade," Don said. "He's the guy you have to thank for getting us out."

We took opportunities to shake his hand. I looked around at the hotel. It was bigger and nicer than any hotel I had ever expected to stay in, with large chandeliers that hung from the ceiling and a wide, spiral, felted staircase. It was without a doubt fancy, but anything would do.

After a brief conversation, a woman led us upstairs to the rest of the group we had gone down to Haiti with. As we walked toward the room, I couldn't help but eye up the food cart parked in the hallway. Just looking at the sandwiches and pastries made my stomach need and my saliva race, but I held back until they filled us in on the situation.

The room looked like it was used for conferences. A few tables surrounded by large chairs formed a circle, each hosting a twirling cabled-phone in the center. A television in the corner was showing footage of the aftermath of the earthquake, not something I wanted to be reminded of. Rubble. People wearing masks and toothpaste under their noses. Helicopters. Diggers moving rubble. People digging through the ruins of a house. "The search for survivors continues..." Someone on the T.V. said.

The Quest group, who had been talking, stood up and hugged us, while the ones on the phone gave a wave or a smile, still deep in what looked like emotional conversations. We had only been separated for a short time, but it felt much longer.

As we sat down, the person who we had been following introduced herself. If she had beforehand, I hadn't noticed.

"Hi, my name is Sandra. I'm sure all of you are excited to be back in Canada. We're here to help you. There are phones here for anyone who wants to call their family. Feel free to talk for as long you want. There's also some food outside in the hallway. I'm just going to ask you to wait a moment before you make any phone calls or eat to allow our psychologist to briefly introduce herself. Someone will come around and give you a key to your room. Thank you for your time and now, if you could listen up to the psychologist, Ms. Carlson."

The psychologist stepped forward, she had a calming demeanor to her. I don't know what it was about her, but she looked like someone who could help me with my feelings of stress and heaviness.

"Hi everybody," Mrs. Carlson said. "I realize you have been through a lot over the last few days. I'll be walking around to quickly chat with you on an individual basis to see how everybody's doing. Anything that you say to me will be confidential."

As soon as she stopped talking, my mom picked up the phone, called the school and asked to speak with our sister. Our mom was crying as she told Taya she loved her. I couldn't hear what Taya was saying, but I could hear that there wasn't much talk.

Skye and I grabbed sandwiches. They were like no sandwich I had before. Each bite brought a lot more than just food. A sense of security. A feeling of safety. It meant we were home.

Ms. Carlson greeted us.

"How are you doing?"

"I'm alright," I said. It felt relieving being back, but there was also a heavy feeling all over my body that wasn't going away.

"Okay. Well, if you ever need to talk, I'm just at the end of the hall." She gave me a room number.

"Thanks."

Eventually, I got on the phone to talk with Taya. It was good to hear her voice. She spoke seldomly as she was sobbing violently on the other end. The twelve-year-old told me she loved me and missed me. I told her the same.

"I can't wait to see you," she said. "I miss you so much."

"You too, TayTay. I love you."

After talking to our sister, Skye and I called our dad at his house.

"It's good to hear you," he said.

"Yeah. It's nice to hear you, too."

"I knew you guys would be okay."

"I miss you," I said.

"Miss you too."

When all of us were finished talking my mom, Ryan, Skye and I set out to find our rooms. There were two rooms, each with two beds.

"Skye or Owen, come with me," our mom said.

Skye and I wanted to be together and we knew it without speaking. But we knew that Ryan and our mom wouldn't share a room.

"I don't know what to do," I said, looking at Skye.

"Well, I'll take this room," Ryan said. "And Cathy'll take that room. Then you two decide where you're going."

Before Skye even suggested anything, we both knew that we wanted to be with Ryan over our mom. We didn't want to leave him alone.

"Wanna just share a bed in Ryan's room?" Skye asked me.

"Yeah, I don't care. Let's do it."

"Really guys?" my mom asked looking at both of us. I could tell she was hurt. She was right next door, but nobody wants to be alone.

"Okay bye," my mom said.

"Sorry mum." Skye said.

We went into our separate rooms.

"I'm taking a shower," Ryan said.

As he showered, Skye and I sat on our bed, not talking. I thought about what I needed. In Haiti, I had needed food, sleep, and a shower. I had already slept on the plane and eaten two sandwiches. Taking a shower would be nice, but it would only make me feel a little better. I needed to feel a lot better after everything that had happened.

The solution to feeling a lot better crossed my mind. As it did, I tried to push it away; it wasn't something I wanted to do. But the more I thought about it, the more I realized that it was a good idea.

I needed to cry.

Ryan got out of the shower. I stood up and stared at the bed, thinking about crying. But as much as I thought about it, no tears were surfacing. Maybe I couldn't cry. Maybe it just wasn't going to happen.

We left the room together to find more of Quest. "I'll be right back," I said to the guys as I headed toward the phone room. I didn't tell them why I was going. I didn't want them to know I was going to cry. I didn't want to seem weak.

I headed to the phone room to find the psychologist. All I needed to do was find her. She would make me cry.

They know how to do that stuff.

Close to the conference room was a small room with a computer inside. Aubray and Katie stood leaning over, looking at the screen as Brooklyn sat at the computer. All of them were evidently clean from showering.

"Hey guys, do you know where the psychologist's room is?" I asked, hastily. I wanted to hurry up and get it over with.

"Why do you need her?" Katie asked.

"Uhh..." I paused, unsure if I wanted to tell them. "'Cause I need to cry." I admitted, embarrassed.

Smiles formed on all three of the girls faces. "Aww," Aubray teased in the friendly way that she always did.

"Why don't you just cry then?" Katie asked.

"I can't," I said.

"Yes you can," Aubray said.

"I tried. I can't," I said.

"Just do it," Katie said.

"I can't. I just can't." I could feel the emotions creeping up slowly. I tried to be hostile toward the feelings. Anything was better than crying.

"Look, here's how it is. When I left Haiti, I needed three things: food, sleep, and a shower. I slept on the plane, I ate some sandwiches, and then I tried crying, but I couldn't. That's why I need the psychologist, 'cause she'll be able to make me cry. They know how to do that stuff," I said.

Aubray laughed and said, "You don't need the psychologist to help you cry. Just cry!"

She moved to hug me, putting her head against my chest. Katie followed. As their arms wrapped around me, the emotions surfaced. The tears flowed. Brooklyn grabbed my hand from where she sat, squeezing it. I could feel the guilt and emptiness leaving me. We could have done more to help them. We had left so many people behind. We had seen things but did nothing about it. Nothing. The tears stopped.

"Thanks guys. I needed that," I said.

The three of them continued to hold on to me for another moment, eventually letting me break away. I smiled at them as I wiped my cheeks.

"You ate, and you slept," Aubray asked. "Have you showered yet?" She gave me a look like she could tell I hadn't when we embraced. I shook my head. We laughed together.

"Thanks guys." I said.

"Any time, Owen."

I left the room, feeling the weight of a heavy blanket lifted from my body. Almost like everything was all over. I went into the washroom to clean up the evidence of tears. As I washed my face, I got a good look at myself. It was the first time in a week I had looked in a mirror.

Beneath my brown eyes, some bags had formed. My brown, stubbly beard was tipped with a little unexpected orange. I touched my belly I could tell I had lost a little weight, but I felt heavier. I felt older.

I left the washroom and headed back toward my room when I saw Ryan and Skye.

"Hey," Skye said.

"Hey."

"We've been looking for you," Skye said.

"Oh yeah. Why?" I asked.

"We're going to get some clean clothes from Zellers" Ryan informed me. As we walked down to the main lobby, they filled me in.

The company had given those of us that didn't have clean clothes two-hundred dollar gift cards. Whatever we didn't spend, we could keep or return to Zellers.

The store was a couple blocks away. It was a giant of a store, but relatively empty. Which I was happy for. I didn't want to be around people.

Zellers was cheap, I could have gotten a lot with two-hundred dollars. I was wearing sandals, a t-shirt, jeans, and to top it all off, my big puffy winter jacket. I grabbed a t-shirt.

"Is that all you're getting?" Elijah asked as he pushed a shopping cart that was already starting to fill up.

"Yeah, I don't need anything else," I said.

"Dude," Elijah said. "Get a pair of shorts. There's a hot tub back at the hotel." He laughed. I grinned.

I liked that idea, grabbing a pair of shorts. Shoes would be too much of a hassle. It was always difficult getting shoes, as my feet varied in size by half a measurement, and it didn't help that they had a different shape to each other. I didn't want to spend the time finding shoes. My mind was too clouded to shop for that long. I bought the shirt, giving the store clerk the gift card afterward. I don't think any of us planned on keeping the vouchers, we knew other people needed them.

After shopping and bringing our new clothes up to the rooms, Don called us together for a meeting in the hotel lobby. Once we got comfy, he began.

"I called this meeting because I've noticed something, not in all of you, but in many. I think we're getting caught up in the media. They're all over us and we're excited about that, but we have to remember it is Haiti that matters. We owe the Haitians, especially Haiti Arise, and we cannot forget that. They made sacrifices for us.

"Whenever you talk to the media, you must end with Haiti. End with the idea that they need help, not with the idea of us. Always end with the idea of Haiti.

"We're getting too caught up in the fame, but we must realize that people will forget all about us and all about Haiti. It'll be tough for us, especially for Marc and the Haitians. Next time you talk to a news anchor, remember to mention Haiti Arise, or even mention their website." He put in a final word of encouragement, "We'll be home tomorrow, so hang in there everyone. You're doing well. I'm really proud of you." His voice had softened a lot.

As Don stopped, Nicole enthusiastically chimed in, "That's such a good point! Yeah, Don! Let's have a big group hug!" We cheered with her as we moved in for a big embrace.

"Alright! Let's go eat!" Don shouted as he led the way to the dining room.

What Don had said was true. I liked the idea of being a "celebrity." Don was right. On the way to get clothes, I had imagined us going on the Oprah show, or a movie being created about us. The weird thing was that in Haiti, I hadn't gone off into fantasies. In Haiti, I had been preoccupied with everything happening around me, but since I felt safe, I started to think about fame and Oprah.

We entered the dining room, and if there had been any thoughts other than food, they were washed away. The dining room was massive, looking like it served huge banquets or weddings or conferences. Some of the survivors were already eating.

The dinner was buffet style, each dish a traditional Haitian one; fish with pasta, yellow colored rice with beans, more beans and more rice. Most of us sat down in a hurry and shoveled down food. When there was talk, it was short, and through mouths. At the end of it, I felt like my stomach was going to burst.

After dinner, Ryan, Skye and I made our way upstairs, changing for the hot tub. By the time we made it to the pool, Bryden, Cam, Elijah, Jon, and Kyler were already relaxing, letting the bubbles overtake them. It was all the boys, except for Blake, who I could only assume was with Rachel.

The water was soothingly warm, and made it's best attempt to relax my tense body. My legs floated lightly. Every so often, I pushed them down with my arms, or readjusted my seating to plant them back on the hot tub floor. It reminded me of the back of the truck in Haiti, when we were delivering rice. I couldn't keep my legs down, except that had been much harder. This was slow, and almost therapeutic.

"Hey Ryan, where are your water wings?" Cam joked.

"I forgot them at lifeguard school." Ryan said.

After a good soak, we went our separate ways to bed. I'm sure some of the group woke up at four in the morning, but as the three of us got to our bedroom, we were ready to pass out. Even though there wasn't much room to spread out because I shared the bed with my brother, I was astonished by the comfort of it. It had been a while since I had slept in a real bed. Tomorrow, we were heading home and that brought me comfort as well, but what I didn't realize was how different home would be.

13. A Different Home

Around me, everything was shaking, in an unexpected aftershock. I held on to my seat tightly gripping at the armrest that was so often argued over. My classmates were reacting the same, clenching their seats, holding their breaths, waiting for it to finish. A rush of fear ran through my body. The turbulence of the airplane subsided, and I looked over at my brother beside me. Every one of us had noticed that the turbulence was wildly similar to a minor aftershock.

We landed in Calgary, because that's as far as West Jet could take us. It was there that, we said goodbye to Marc. Each of us took turns hugging him, thanking him for everything he had done for us. From Calgary we caught a bus. It was late in the evening when we arrived, but this was it, we were home. We walked off the bus, single file. The principal held the door open to the school, tears in his eyes.

The school was full of relatives, friends, teachers, some students, and even a few news teams. A lot of people ran into hugs.

Immediately, I spotted out my sister and dad, and to my surprise, they were with other relatives. My aunt, cousin, and grandma had come from Vancouver. Without hesitation, my mom ran forward, grabbing my sister and hugging her. The two of them refused to let each other go.

Skye and I took turns hugging each of them while my mom continued to embrace Taya. My dad stood back, smiling at Skye and I as he let the others hug us first. When my mom finally let Taya go, I grabbed her. As we hugged, tears streamed down her face.

"I love you, Tay."

"I love you, too," she said. "I missed you."

After the initial meetings with family, we went to talk with other people. No boundaries existed that night. Parents whom I had never met before hugged me and people I had never seen before shook my hand. I approached Brooklyn's mom and dad. Her mom hugged me.

Her dad shook my hand and said, "Anyone who has been through something like that with my daughter is considered family."

Don hoisted himself on to a bench, standing tall afterward. Instantly, the few reporters in the school surrounded him. When he had grabbed everyone's attention, he spoke.

"To quote Martin Luther King Jr. he said, 'The ultimate measure of a man is not where he stands in moments of comfort and convenience, but where he stands at times of challenge and controversy.' The Haitian's did not know where they stood, but still helped us, fed us, sheltered us. It's one thing to be generous and gracious when you are secure, but when your whole country has been devastated, it's really telling of the people."

He continued to talk about the sacrifices the people at Haiti Arise had made. "They did so much to help us, even when they needed help themselves."

After all the hugs, tears and smiles, the school cleared out. Each and every one of us wanted to get home after all.

"Alright, see ya guys this weekend," my dad said.

Wait what?

He was leaving? I thought he would've gone to my mom's place to talk with us. I got that he hadn't been to my mom's house since their divorce three years earlier, but I figured this would have changed things.

As we drove, I looked at where I had grown up. The place that I call home. The trees still littered the mountains, the river beside the highway still flowed and the snow still fell in large quantities, but somehow it didn't feel the same. I had expected arriving home to bring a sense of comfort, but it didn't. I just felt lost. Lost, even in my own home.

Opening the door, we were greeted by our dog. He jumped at us excitedly, missing us as much as he did every day, no matter the circumstance.

"I missed you too, Chile," I said, rubbing his head.

My mom started up the kettle to make some tea, and then all of us sat down in the living room to talk. Taya cuddled up close to my mom, not saying a word as we tried to talk a little. She didn't let her go for the entire evening. It was mainly my mom speaking, and she barely touched on what happened. She seemed to dance around the subject.

"In time," my Aunt said. "There's no rush."

Taya didn't let go of my mom. She just kept holding her arm and saying nothing.

The next morning, we had an early meeting with the Quest group. In the room was the school's guidance counselor, Don and the rest of the group. Even though we had only been separated for a couple of days, it was good to see everyone. But my friends looked different. The bags under their eyes had disappeared and some of the girls had straightened or curled their hair and the boys had styled theirs, with the exception of Elijah, whose hair was still wild. It seemed like each was trying to look his or her best, as if to show that they were back. As if they were already over Haiti.

"I'm sure all of you have heard of Post Traumatic Stress Disorder," the counselor said. "Or PTSD, for short. I want you all to be keeping an eye out for the signs. Don't be afraid to speak to me if you need someone to talk to. While we can talk here, the school will also pay for any counseling services you request outside of here. I know it has a stigma attached to it, but go anyways. PTSD is not something you want to mess around with," the counselor concluded.

I didn't know much about PTSD, but I knew I didn't have it. That was the shit soldiers got after 'Nam where they just stared at an empty T.V. screen, reliving the horrors in their own heads.

Our group was finished. Nicole was leaving school early, Jodie moved to a different school, and Katie went away for a volleyball program. The rest of us began the final semester of a senior year that was unlike any other.

At school, it felt like everything had changed. In the time we had left, new relationships started, old ones ended, and school itself felt strange. Normally, I did well in class and liked school well enough, but after Haiti, all I wanted was for the weekend to come. I didn't know what Friday would bring, but it would mean I had made it through one more week. By the end of the first week, I had already dropped a course.

That night I had my first nightmare about Haiti.

In my dream, I was standing in a graveyard. A thick fog hung over the area, making it hard to see, but even with my limited vision I recognized the place. It was the graveyard from *The Serpent and The Rainbow*. A Haitian man was there with me. He was on his knees with a look of horror and pain on his face, yelling something I couldn't make out, but I knew a terrible thing had taken place.

His scream was overwhelming, piercing, and growing with every moment. I covered my ears, but it amplified the scream. It was going through my hands, directly into my ears, louder than any sound I had heard before. I wanted to help him. I did. I stepped closer, but the closer I got, the more my attitude started to switch. I began to laugh at the man. I was laughing as he screamed a horrible scream. He was suffering. He needed my help, but I couldn't stop laughing.

I jerked out of the dream, sitting up on the top bunk. I peaked down at the bottom bed, half hoping that Skye was awake. He wasn't. I didn't need to look at the clock to assume the time.

It has to be four in the morning. That's when they always hit.

Still startled by the dream, I sat up as much as my top bunk permitted. I didn't want to go back to sleep—not to that, not to Haiti.

Each of us had a newly found heightened sense of awareness following the earthquake.

Sudden movements and noises that previously meant nothing had become potentially life threatening. What had formerly gone unnoticed became dreaded. The shaking of washing machines, the rumble of a nearby passing train or even the slight movement of someone stomping their foot nearby brought any one of us to believe that an earthquake was about to hit. Running from movement or loud noises had become instinctual. All of us were jumpy.

Everything reminded me of Haiti, even the screaming and crying of people in movies. The saying "on solid ground" was worthless. Nothing more than stale air.

"Earthquake" had now become the most recognizable word in the English language. It showed up in conversation, articles, and especially in songs. All of a sudden, it seemed like earthquakes were happening all over the world —Chile, Ecuador, Indonesia. And Haiti's earthquake had not finished.

The number of people Haiti lost during the disaster was greatly disputed, ranging from a hundred thousand people, which is widely sought as more accurate, upwards to three-hundred thousand. There were over a million people homeless or displaced. And two days after we left, the earthquake that we so feared hit. It had been less powerful than the original, but still took its toll. The following October, there was a massive outbreak of Cholera. Due to the amount of deaths and instability, there wasn't a solid government in power until the next year. The country was still suffering, and I was doing everything I could to forget it.

But, deep down, I knew I could never forget what happened in Haiti. I could never forget the child wrapped in the blood soaked blanket.

Spears

Owen Spears was born in Ottawa, Ontario but grew up in Vancouver and Nelson, B.C. before following his partner over to Ireland, where he has spent the last couple years. An extremely premature birth resulted in him having cerebral palsy, restrictive lung function and hearing loss, but he doesn't let the challenges hold him back from travelling or writing. He also likes to bike (it has stabilizers) and go for moderate hikes.

Printed in Great Britain
by Amazon

34950331R00097